RAILWAY GHOSTS AND PHANTOMS

RAILWAY GHOSTS
AND PHANTOMS

W. B. HERBERT

GUILD PUBLISHING

LONDON · NEW YORK · SYDNEY · TORONTO

TO MY MOTHER

This edition published 1989 by Guild Publishing
by arrangement with David & Charles

CN 1361

Printed in Great Britain
by Billings & Son Ltd, Worcester
for David & Charles Publishers plc
Brunel House   Newton Abbot   Devon

CONTENTS

FOREWORD

Nothing – but nothing – is quite as atmospheric as a railway: a village's link with the outside world, a country station where an only son set off for war, a bustling terminus where the grand and the bland go about their travels. So it follows that it throws up ghosts – of journeys past, of lovers gone, of children emigrated, of work done, and of prisoners returned.

Hustle, toil, noise, steam, smoke, joy, despair, honeymoons, deaths – all are entwined and encompassed by railways, on lines both extant and extinct.

Whether you believe in actual ghosts, as assuredly as does the author, or (like me) sense that such a tumult of human and mechanical experience in often otherwise unremarkable settings gives rise to a tangible atmosphere, it matters not: the stories collected by Barry Herbert deserve to be shared with a wider audience.

It is no coincidence that a good many are set in one of the least known and most potentially ethereal corners of England, Lincolnshire. A county of low cold mists, treeless fieldscapes, bleak coastal marshes, hidden wold villages and the windswept quays of Immingham and New Holland, Grimsby and Boston. A county whose railway lines and stations are steeped in time and history.

Whether the overgrown remains of the Lincolnshire Coast Light Railway near the author's home at Humberston, the ploughed-in trackbed of the now vanished Midland and Great Northern Joint line at Whaplode, or the record-breaking 'Mallard's' racetrack on Stoke Bank, they still exude ghosts.

I promise that you will not forget any of these ghostly tales of the tracks.

CHRIS BATES 1989

1

THE BRIGHT LIGHT

On the evening of 25 October 1919, John MacDonald spent a few hours with his friend Jim Jackson at Berryburn Croft in the hills of Dunphail. At about 11.30pm he left Berryburn on his bicycle and cycled the 3 miles to Bogney railway crossing where he could travel along the pathway beside the railway line. The moon was so full that it was almost like daylight. He continued on his way until he came to the deep cutting just below Achanlochen where he lived with his grandmother. Then, before his very eyes appeared the brightest light he had ever seen. He got off his bicycle and stood for a while trying to discover the cause of the brilliance. Eventually, however, it faded until the only light that remained was the moonlight that bathed the hills in its natural glow.

The next morning John MacDonald returned to the place where he had been mystified the previous night. He searched the area for clues, but could find no answer to the mystery. He told the foreman, Mr Calder, of his experience and he, too, had seen the light on the line when he was walking along the path late that night. He learned that several other people had shared the experience and were convinced that it was a sign, perhaps from the supernatural world.

No answer could be found to explain the mystery of the bright light and from that day John MacDonald never walked along the old track-bed from Dunphail to Dava.

This same railway line was the subject of another mysterious happening a few years earlier. In December 1917, when the ground was covered by a thick hard crust of snow, John MacDonald was returning home on the path beside the railway at about 8pm when there appeared high in the sky beside the Plough stars an engine and four trucks containing cattle. He could see the trucks moving and smoke coming from the engine. Mr Calder and John's Uncle Angus, who had a large farm at Kerrow in that area, also saw the ghostly train and could give no explanation, apart from the fact that a train of forty cattle-filled trucks had burned at Dava Station about thirty years earlier and all the cattle had died.

2

THE MYSTERY OF DUNSTER
GOODS SHED

The goods shed at Dunster, on the now reawakened West Somerset Railway, is the subject of a ghostly presence. The phenomenon takes the shape of a black shadow that moves about in the dark corners of the old cavernous shed in a menacing way startling anyone who happens to be in the area at the time. Apparently, a shunter was killed inside the shed many years ago and it is believed that it is his ghost who haunts the shed looking for his train.

Few people who have witnessed the apparition are prepared to share their experience, so perhaps it is one story where it is best to let sleeping ghosts rest in peace.

3

THE MOTH THAT SAVED
QUEEN VICTORIA'S LIFE

A man visited the Natural History Museum in London and after looking around the show cases and exhibits, he enquired about the moth that saved Queen Victoria's life. To the nonplussed staff he explained the following story that he had heard and the reason that he wanted to see the moth.

One summer, Queen Victoria was travelling by train with Benjamin Disraeli to Balmoral for her holiday. Towards evening, when darkness was closing in, the train suddenly ground to a halt. The Queen immediately sent Disraeli to find out the reason for the unscheduled stop.

Treading carefully in the ballast beside the track, the statesman approached the engine. The driver, recognising Disraeli's aristocratic bearing but perhaps not his role in this unusual incident, explained that the train had stopped because he had seen a figure dancing on the line. Being very perceptive, Disraeli beckoned the driver to the front of the engine and showed him the object that most likely had caught his attention. A large moth had been attracted to one of the headlights — probably the heat had drawn it on to the glass, thus giving the effect of movement. Disraeli caught the moth and put it in a handkerchief, perhaps intending to show the creature to the Queen later.

Owing to this stop, the royal party's arrival at Ballater was delayed, but at the next signal box a message was passed to the driver that a tree had fallen across the track further along the line. Perhaps the moth had played a part in slowing down the royal train, thus allowing warning to be given and safety measures to be taken to protect the train and its important passengers.

4

EXTRACTS FROM
OUR HAUNTED KINGDOM

Bank Station

Rail workers at Bank Station complain of a pungent smell normally associated with open graves and as a plague pit is believed to be situated nearby it could explain the unpleasant odour that pervades the air.

The ghost of Sarah Whitehead has been seen in the Bank of England's garden. Sarah was the sister of an employee of the bank who was caught forging cheques in 1811 and he was subsequently sentenced to death for what was then a major felony. Sarah's mind broke with distress and for the rest of her life she visited Bank Station looking for her brother. On her sudden death she was buried in an old graveyard which was eventually destroyed to form one of the entrances to the station.

Ickenham Station

At 2am on 2 March 1951 a London Transport engineer working at the end of the down platform at Ickenham Station, near Uxbridge, happened to see an incredible sight which he would never forget, for his eyes alighted on the ghost of a middle-aged woman wearing a red scarf beckoning him to the huge switchboard on which he was working. The ghost indicated that he should follow her down the staircase. At that moment he did not realise that she was a ghostly creature and prepared to follow her bidding. However, she suddenly vanished from sight when she reached the last step on the stairway. The engineer still did not realise that he had been following a ghost and continued to look around for her. When he had searched everywhere to no avail he realised that he had seen a ghost at first hand.

Several other railway workers have also seen this ghost. Apparently, she fell on a conductor rail many years ago and occasionally she returns to the station to the scene of her fatal accident.

Watford Railway Tunnel

When the London & Birmingham Railway was constructing the railway near Watford and was excavating the land to bore Watford tunnel, they had to bore through part of a church-yard. Coffins were exposed and considerable embarrassment was felt by the contractors as they had no prime intention of disturbing the dead. Remains of the corpses fell on the workers who naturally felt both horrified and frightened by their un-pleasant experience.

When the line and tunnel were completed, the trains ran without any problem, until the occurrence of a phenomenon at Watford tunnel. The footplate crews found that every time they fired their locomotives near the tunnel there was a vicious blow-back from the fire-box with the result that several drivers and firemen were badly burned. An investigation showed that this incident always occurred when the engine was directly beneath the churchyard and the train crews sur-mised that it was the dead taking their revenge on the railway for disturbing their eternal peace.

5

THE DWARF'S APPARITION

A husband and wife were travelling along the railway from Ipswich some years ago and as they passed a church by the railway, the lady became aware of a curious apparition which seemed to come up through the middle of the carriage floor. It was a dwarf-like man, dressed in peasant's clothing. He was crouching and looked up at the church as the train passed by it, then he disappeared into the floor again. The husband was not aware of the incident and his wife said nothing about it to him at the time except to ask him the name of the place that they had just passed. He told her that it was called Haughley. She had only travelled over that stretch of line two or three times but her husband, an engine driver, had worked trains over it many times. Later she asked him if he had had any unusual experiences on that line, but he said that he had not. He did not believe in ghosts and would not have believed what his wife had seen. For his wife, who believes she is psychic, the apparition was unforgettable. The dwarf's dress was probably about two hundred or three hundred years old.

The lady had another curious experience many years ago. Her husband came home from work at all hours so she always kept the back door unlocked for his return. One night at about 2am she was awakened by somebody telling her that she had locked the back door and her husband would not be able to get in. Although she was almost asleep, she had to make sure. In fact, she had absent-mindedly locked and bolted it. She undid the door, went back to bed and a few minutes later her husband came home.

The husband was working with Jimmy Knightall the day before the contents of a munitions train exploded. Jimmy had said to her husband, 'I have a feeling that I'm not going to live much longer.' The next day he was killed in the blast at Soham.

6

HAUNTINGS AT THE
ELEPHANT & CASTLE

The Elephant & Castle Underground Station used to be haunted by mysterious running footsteps, knockings, tappings, and a self-opening door. Mrs G. C. Watson of Herne Hill was travelling home late one night. The only passenger on the platform, she was impressed by the eerie silence of the station. She saw a porter coming towards her and mentioned to him how still and silent the old building was. The porter agreed and said that several ghosts frequented the station. He told her of several frightening experiences that he had witnessed and he was not anxious to repeat them. On night-shift he usually spent most of his duty in the porter's room with the door firmly closed, but to his horror on several occasions the door had swung open on its own. He had looked to see who had opened the door thinking that one of his mates had played a practical joke on him, but there was nobody in sight. This strange occurrence happened several times without any rational explanation. He often heard tapping noises and the sound of running footsteps, but again no reason could be found to explain them. His mate who worked the other shift also heard the strange noises, but on investigation no reason was evident. The ghostly sounds were heard mostly on winter nights and footsteps were also heard on the stairway which at the time was deserted.

A porter at Blackfriars, Mr Horton, refused to work night-shifts at the Elephant & Castle after one night's duties in the porter's room when he had heard running footsteps. Mr Horton also had the frightening experience of hearing footsteps halting outside the porter's room, then two taps sounding on the door. In terror Mr Horton opened the door but the platform was empty.

On Saturday nights the station was locked up but passers-by were still surprised to hear the sound of running footsteps.

7

EXTRACTS FROM
GHOSTS OF NORTH–WEST ENGLAND

Waterfoot

The Railway Inn at Waterfoot, near Rochdale, is believed to be haunted by a tall lady dressed in grey who appeared in a particular bedroom and walked through a partition wall. She was known as 'Jane' by the licencees and blamed for interfering with bedclothes by pulling them completely off the bed. A bricked up room has been associated with the ghostly occurrences, although there is nothing unusual or macabre in the room.

Mayfield Railway Station

Although now used as a parcel depot, for twenty years Mayfield Station in Greater Manchester was a terminus and shunting yard. A dilapidated building of crumbling walls, rusty ironwork, cobwebs, broken roofs and decaying platforms, it was the ideal setting for a ghostly experience, especially on a wild winter's night. In its more active days, the then foreman Fred Jenks knew that a man had hanged himself in the electric indicator box and that a former station foreman had hanged himself in the station lavatory. Also, a night workman had opened the baggage hoist thinking the lift was at his level and he had fallen 50ft to his death down the shaft. Fred Jenks heard footsteps on three occasions, passing the foreman's office and continuing towards the baggage hoist, but he never saw anyone on the deserted platform. Porter Ted Dyson, a tall tough man, said, 'I was sitting here alone when suddenly I felt a prickly feeling up my spine, then I heard the footsteps.' Shunter Charlie Movey also had a similar experience. At about 3 o'clock one morning he was about to go off duty and heard footsteps close behind him; about a fortnight later he heard them again. He flooded the platform with light by switching on every light as light usually gives courage in times of stress. He looked everywhere but could find no explanation for the mysterious events; the sound of the ghostly footsteps seemed to pass very close, then within seconds they ceased.

To this day no explanation has been found to solve the mystery of this strange sequence of events that has puzzled everyone who knows the old building and has worked in or around the station complex.

8

THE FOOTPLATE GHOST

The following story is told by a retired railwayman and his experience occurred at around the turn of the century.

I was driving the 8.30 train to the North and left King's Cross four minutes behind time. I can't tell you what it was, but I never felt nervousness but once on an engine, and that was on the night I'm talking about.

Now, sir, I don't know nothing about ghosts or spirits or apparitions — call 'em what you like — but I'm ready to swear before any judge today that I saw something of the kind that night, and no amount of argument will change my belief. It was just when we were passing through Hatfield Town when, I would take my oath for all I am worth, that a man stepped from the platform to the footplate, just as easily as though we weren't travelling about 55mph. I can see his face and dress to this day. It was the saddest face I have ever seen. The eyes seemed to look right through you and he was dressed all in black. I never felt so terrified in my life.

The curious thing is that Dick, my fireman, saw nothing at all. He coaled up for the hill by Welwyn just as natural as though all was fair sailing, and when I tried to shout to him, I felt a great lump in my throat and not a word could I speak. I soon noticed that the stranger never went to any other part of the footplate except to the spot where I stood, and he even edged up so close to me that I went cold all over. My feet were like lumps of ice. I think I must have acted mechanically for I watched the man put his hand on the regulator. I put my hand on his and the touch of his hand was like ice, but I couldn't loosen his grip and before I realised it steam was being shut off and we were slowing down. Dick, my fireman, must have thought I was mad. He had been up on the tender breaking up coal. He came down and craned his neck to see why we had shut off steam, then he saw as I did that the distant signal was off and after that the home signal stood for line clear. You wouldn't believe it perhaps, but it is the gospel truth that though I knew the way was clear I felt compelled to stop the train and stop her I did just outside Hitchin Station.

For nothing, you say. Well, heaven alone knows how, but it proved to be for a great deal. There were two trucks across the main line and although the signals were off, the way was blocked so that me and the passengers behind me wouldn't be living to tell the story if I hadn't been helped by the cold man who stepped into the cab and shut off steam.

9

BARKSTON SOUTH SIGNAL BOX

One midsummer night in 1961 Mr P. Handford intended to make some sound recordings on the East Coast main line in the Grantham area — the exact location was to depend on the weather. In the early evening he called at Grantham Station to talk to an inspector he knew there and told him that he had decided to go to Barkston Junction and spend the night there. He asked the inspector for relevant information on possible traffic.

It was dusk when he arrived at Barkston Junction, parked the car and walked around to decide on the best position for his microphones and other equipment. The South Box was in darkness which did not surprise Mr Handford as he had been told at Grantham that it would be switched out from 10pm. What did surprise him was that the door was open so he walked over to the box thinking that plans might have been changed or that he had been misinformed. He went into the box and said good evening to the signalman who sat inside gazing out of the window with his back to him. The signalman was startled to see Mr Handford who explained the purpose of his visit, showed him his permit and asked his opinion on traffic prospects for the night so far as steam workings were concerned. The signalman seemed strangely disinterested and uncommunicative and started to talk about a girl who had recently been murdered in nearby woods by a man who was still at large. This was a complete surprise because murders at that time were rare enough to be widely publicised and Mr Handford had not heard of any such happening, especially in the Barkston area. He did not stay more than a few minutes. There seemed little point in doing so and he wanted to get his equipment set up as it was about 10.45pm and nearly dark.

During a long night's recording he looked across at the signal box from time to time but at no time was it lit up and all the signals under its control were permanently off. By 5am he had to abandon recording because of wind and rain, so he packed up his equipment and prepared to leave. Before departing, however, he walked across to the South Box and found it deserted with the door locked.

Later in the morning when Mr Handford called at Grantham Station he was again told that the Barkston South Box was unmanned during that midsummer night. Who then was the signalman?

10

THE HAYLING ISLAND GHOST

Mr S. Winser of Purbrook, Hampshire, recalled a newspaper article dated 30 October 1980 that tells of the unexplained hauntings at the old disused Hayling Island Station. The branch was closed on 4 November 1963 after nearly one hundred years of service to the local community. A quaint line, nicknamed the 'Hayling Billy', the line was well used in early post-war years, but like many others it found that progress meant more cars and the local branches were being forsaken and in many cases closed in the teeth of opposition from the new generation of travellers.

The service usually consisted of a Stroudley 'Terrier' Class 0–6–0 tank locomotive built in the late 1870s and still capable of running a service. This class of engine was originally used on several Southern branch lines. The engine on the Hayling Island branch usually hauled one non-corridor coach as this formation was considered adequate for the number of passengers using the service. After closure of the branch line and the attempts to erase every sign of a railway, all that remained was the goods shed and platform at the southern terminus. The local council once used the area as a storage yard for its vans and other equipment, but now the site is disused and abandoned, although the track-bed is used by horse-riders and walkers. The goods shed is in surprisingly good condition and still displays its Southern Railway paint, albeit rather faded now but still defiantly showing the old company flag (one wonders why this attractive little line was not the subject of an attempt at private preservation). As dereliction set in and the weeds strengthened their hold on the track-bed, the Hayling Billy became forgotten in the minds of the local people, but to some people the memory lingered on in a very strange way.

In March 1969 a Havant Council workman and a Southern Electricity Board fitter had been working in the old station on routine jobs when they encountered a ghost. One of these two gentlemen stated that he turned round to find a pair of legs behind him, but when he struggled to his feet, the figure, wearing black boots and faded trousers, disappeared. Another council workman recalled that while working at a desk something grabbed his arm; he jumped to his feet but there was nothing to be seen. After their accounts appeared in a local newspaper, Mrs Elsie Taylor of Elm Grove, Hayling, claimed that the ghost was that of her late father, Jack Wilkinson, who had worked at the station for about thirty years. Mr Wilkinson had boasted that he would never die as long as the Hayling Billy rolled along the tracks. In 1947 he died, but apparently he was loathe to leave the scene of his earthly toil.

One man who recalls a strange incident at the station is Henry Cutting of Langstone. He had been visiting his wife's parents in West Town and decided to take a walk along the old railway line with his dog. Entering the station environs he wandered round the old crumbling buildings and eventually came to the little ticket office. 'I was thinking how wonderful it must have been in the old days when the old Billy was running', said Mr Cutting. He tugged at the lead but his dog would not enter the building. Its hair stood on end and the animal was plainly distressed. Mr Cutting had never seen his pet behave like this before and he was very perplexed. He tugged the lead again but the dog refused to move. Undeterred, he dropped the lead and entered the building and looked around. Nothing untoward met his gaze except the usual scene of decay evident in an abandoned ticket office. His dog remained outside.

He left the station and returned home and told his father-in-law about his experience. 'No wonder', his father-in-law replied. 'That's the room the old station master died in. It was his office and they say he *never* left it.' So the restless ghost of the station master still remains on duty and is perhaps happy in his old habitat doing nobody any harm.

It is common knowledge that animals are more susceptible to paranormal phenomena than man, so we are left with an even stronger case for belief in the story.

11

THE CLAIRVOYANT'S WARNING

Any accident has its interesting features that can be put down
to human error and it is very easy to be wise after the event, but
the case of the accident at Barnetby when a DMU hit a Class 47
on an oil train has the aura of mystery. Unfortunately, in this
incident a 19-year-old girl was killed in the DMU which was
damaged beyond repair. As the subsequent inquiry revealed,
the accident was shrouded in mystery.

The *Grimsby Evening Telegraph* of 17 January 1984 reported
the inquiry as follows.

A power cut to a signal box could have caused December's
fatal rail accident at Wrawby Junction near Barnetby, a
Doncaster inquiry was told yesterday.

47299 IN FATAL ACCIDENT

*The jinx that has haunted an Immingham-based Class 47 for
over 2 years followed it to a remarkable crash at nearby
Barnetby on December 9.*

*After predictions of impending doom, BR even renumbered
47216 to 47299 in December 1981, but it obviously made little
difference.*

*It was hauling an oil train when it collided head-on with a
Cleethorpes-Sheffield Class 114 DMU 53049–54049, leaving one person dead, the diesel unit severely damaged, and both
cabs of 47299 stove in.*

One of the theories put forward for the crash between a two-car diesel multiple unit and an empty oil train was that a set of points had moved on their own, and a British Rail engineer said this could have been caused by a power cut.

Grimsby art student Rachel Taylor (19) of Kirton Lindsey died in the smash and five people were injured. The DMU was travelling from Cleethorpes to Sheffield while the oil train was heading for the Lindsey Oil Terminal at Killingholme.

Signalman Arthur Dennis Day who was on duty at the Wrawby Junction box at the time said he noticed a 'Track Failure' on one of the circuits.

He advised the signalmen at their boxes on either side of him that he was going to crank the points manually, and went out with a flag man to do this.

After cranking them and checking that the points were lying correctly, he went back to his box. Then, after the oil train set off, the collision occurred.

Mr Day said he thought the accident happened because the points moved after he turned his back on them. He thought this might have been caused by the vibration of the oncoming oil train.

Another signalman, Mr Reginald Wilson, said he went off duty from the box before the accident and did not know anything about it until he was told by his son at 10pm.

While on duty there had been no problem with the signalling equipment.

The driver of the passenger train, Mr Harold Faulkener, of Penistone, said he stopped at Wrawby Junction, where the signal was at danger, and then received a hand signal to continue.

He had gone only a few yards when the accident occurred. Mr Faulkener told the inquiry that he saw the freight train on the opposite line, but at the time did not know if it was stationery or moving. The train was travelling at six or seven miles an hour, he said.

His guard, Mr Paul Anthony Vernon, said he was standing beside Mr Faulkener when the accident happened. He was trapped for some time with a girl passenger.

The driver of the oil train, Mr Ambrose Thomas Kirman, said that at the junction he received a green hand signal to move forward and then, seeing a light ahead, sounded his horn. When he had increased speed, his engine veered to the right and the crash happened. It took him two or three minutes to release himself but he was not injured.

The Area Signals Engineer based at Grantham, Mr C. I. Weightman, said his inquiries had revealed that the integrity of the signalling system had not been brought into question. The circuit could have been reset by the public power supply to the signal box being interrupted. If there had been an interruption this could have affected the points.

There is more to the story, however, than was revealed by this factual account.

The freight engine was a Type 47, a reliable class of mixed traffic locomotive used all over the British Railways system. First introduced in 1962, these locomotives could handle any sort of working and were generally popular with the train crews. It is, nevertheless, possible for an unexplained jinx to attach itself to anything and it would appear that something of this nature had affected this particular locomotive. It was said that 47 216 had had more than its fair share of trouble and doubts were being cast on its availability.

Things happened to it that should have never happened. Such a trustworthy class of engines was usually renowned for its time-keeping, trouble-free running and ease of maintenance, but 47 216 was said to be rogue. Although the faults experienced with the locomotive were easily overcome and explained rationally, it gained a bad reputation and was not welcome in some depots.

To add to the mystery, a clairvoyant telephoned a British Rail Headquarters office and asked if they had a Class 47 locomotive. She was told that they had several hundred, but she was asked if she had one particular engine in mind.

No 47 216 was the reply, and the clairvoyant then warned that this locomotive would be involved in a fatal crash. This news was startling enough, but soon after a warning letter was received at the same office.

British Rail officials were concerned and after some discussion they decided to renumber this errant engine 47 299, perhaps wishing to rid the machine of its unsavoury reputation. For a while all was well and there were no further problems with the engine. However, the driver of the DMU waiting for the signal to proceed at Wrawby Junction one cold December day most likely did not know that the locomotive on the empty oil train was being hauled by the now disguised engine No 47 216, running as No 47 299.

These questions must be asked. Do point switches move on their own? What caused the power failure just at that crucial moment? Human error is always a possibility, but what forces were abroad that day that were to result in a fatal accident that fulfilled the clairvoyant's warning? Perhaps we shall never know, but it would seem that a tragedy was to happen whatever precaution was taken.

12

THE MYSTERIOUS INTRUDER

The following story concerns two officers who, while they were on their beat near the railway station in a little East Coast town, took it upon themselves to check the coaching stock parked in the sidings overnight. It was shortly after 2am on a moonlight September night about seven years ago. The two men had shared many duties together and on this occasion had just been to the police station for their refreshment before resuming their foot patrol. Passing the railway station, the two constables noticed a line of stationery coaches near Platform 1 and they decided to check that they were not being used by intruders. All was quiet as they clambered into an open second-class vehicle. They decided not to embark via the platform, but rather to effect entry further down the rake in order to surprise anyone who might be aboard. Once on board they quietly but thoroughly searched the carriages, checking that all doors and windows were tightly closed. There were eight carriages in the rake and all but one were open seconds and the remaining one a brake second.

After satisfying themselves that all was safe and secure, they sat down in one of the coaches and decided to write up their notebooks. All was quiet and still, but suddenly the silence was broken by the sight and sound of the sliding door opening and shutting. The two men leapt to their feet, their powerful torches searching the dark corners of the coach. They again searched the rake of vehicles, even looking under seats, but no one was there. They looked outside to see if there was a fugitive escaping under the bright moonlight.

They knew that they had both seen the sliding door opening and shutting and they were satisfied that when they had first sat in the carriage there was no one on the rake of coaches. They were convinced that they were looking for a vagrant who had used the coaches for shelter, but they had conducted a thorough search and could find no answer to the mysterious intruder.

They examined the sliding door. It was somewhat stiff to move open and spring-loaded to close. Puzzled, the officers tried to form some logical conclusion. They again looked out of the windows on either side. All was still. Shining their torches, they carefully and quietly climbed down on to the gravel and looked on the underside of the vehicles. They re-embarked on to the coach and looked around again, totally bemused by the unexplained mystery.

They were not used to investigating the occult or para-normal, but when they re-examined the facts the thought occurred to them that they were dealing with a ghost. They had examined every inch of the coaches, had opened every lavatory door, looked under every seat. In other words, there was nowhere that a human being could hide from the probing torch and they felt certain that no one had jumped off the coach. It was a mysterious event that appeared to have no explanation.

Fearing ridicule, the two policemen did not tell any of their colleagues about their strange experience. After much thought and consideration, no explanation was ever found, so no one will know whether the door was opened by a mysterious intruder or indeed a ghost.

13

HAUNTINGS AT ADDISCOMBE
CARRIAGE SHEDS

The ghost which appears in the carriage sheds at Addiscombe is well known to most of the staff. The cleaners, shunters, and signalmen, who work through the night, have many interesting stories to relate of their experiences.

The shed (which has four roads) is used to store and clean EMU stock which is used on Charing Cross and Cannon Street peak-hour suburban services, and hence the shed is only empty in the morning and evening peak hours.

At night, the electric stock, when berthed, is usually cut out by the shunter, therefore isolating the vehicles from the third rail. The hand-brakes are always screwed down tightly for safety reasons. However, on some nights the brake compressors are often heard running even though the units are cut out when they enter the shed. On one particular night a cleaner heard the compressors of a train and told the shunter who then went and again cut out the train. Some time later exactly the same thing happened again and the shunter again cut out this troublesome train, but it happened a third time and the man again cut out the train. This time all was quiet for the rest of the night.

Often during the night, carriage doors are heard opening and closing on their own and also the carriage cleaner's trolleys (with which they gain access to the train from ground level) are often 'moved' during the night from where they have been left. These trolleys take some effort to move and they make a considerable and distinctive noise which on these strange occasions has never been heard.

One of the strangest phenomena to happen during the night is the sound of moving trains inside the shed. Normally the sound of a train moving in the shed is a definite rumble, but this is often heard at night even though there are no trains moving in the shed. It would be totally impossible for these trains to move as they are cut out on entry with their hand-brakes tightly screwed down. But strange as it might seem, *all* the signalmen have heard this strange, uncanny sound of a train moving out of the shed at night and many have gone to the shed to see what is going on, only to find everything normal and still. One signalman was so worried about these sounds that he went to the shed and checked every hand-brake to find that every one was wound down.

The shunters and cleaners also have some stories of their own. One evening the shunter and a cleaner were sitting in the mess room having a cup of tea when the door, which was a tight fit, opened and closed. The two men got up quickly and tried to find who had opened the door, but there was nobody about at all.

An apparition was seen by a shunter when he was waiting outside the shed beside the platform sidings. When he saw a figure dressed in grey leaving the sheds and walking along the track towards him, the shunter was extremely frightened. When he saw that the figure's facial features were blurred and vague, he turned to get a better look but suddenly the strange form had disappeared. The shunter had the same experience in the evening and drivers of incoming trains also reported seeing a figure standing beside the tracks outside the shed entrance staff door.

The shed has four roads. However, it is very unusual for any trains to be berthed in road No 4 as shunters and cleaners have reported that it is much colder by road No 4 for no reason. However, a shunter was crushed and killed between two units in the shed while coupling a train on No 4 road. Also a hot-water boiler had exploded killing some shed staff, and a driver, second man and blacksmith were killed when a train ran through the end of the shed crashing into the smithy which was situated behind the shed building.

Nobody is sure how long the shed has been haunted. It was built in 1925 for the South Eastern Electrification Scheme. Mystery surrounds the exact identity of the ghosts, although many people think the main paranormal force is the ghost of the shunter killed in No 4 road.

All the above-mentioned details have been supplied by the signalmen at Addiscombe. Although many doubt the truth of the stories, there is too much corroboration to dismiss the strange tales about Addiscombe out of hand. To date, no reasonable explanation has been forthcoming to dispel the long-standing ghost stories.

Recently, a joke played by a signalman who pretended to be a ghost backfired in a strange way. A trainee was being instructed in the signal box and as part of his training he had to work at night for a week. The signalman from whom he was receiving his instruction and a member of the platform staff decided to play a joke on the trainee. One of the practical jokers was to hide in the shed and the other, after telling the trainee some ghost stories to frighten him, was to take the trains into the shed. They would then bang on the panels of the trains and open and close doors and generally make ghostly noises to frighten the trainee as much as possible. The two men played ghosts for several nights until one night, as they passed the cleaner's lobby, the door handle rattled furiously of its own accord. Upon this, all three quickly left the shed for the signal box, suitably frightened. Obviously, the Addiscombe carriage shed ghost wished to be included in their game.

14

THE CROSSING OF DEATH

The *Peterborough Citizen and Advertiser's* headlines for 1 March 1948 read: 'Six German prisoners-of-war killed. Five injured as engine hits lorry in fog near Conington.' The report read as follows:

> Six German prisoners-of-war from Glatton Camp were killed and five more were injured when a light engine hit a three-ton lorry on this main line crossing over the Peterborough–London line at Conington in dense fog at 7am yesterday [Monday]. Three were fatally injured and three more were killed instantly. The remaining five were admitted to Peterborough Hospital in a serious condition. They were travelling to work at Messrs B. and C. Papworth's Charter Farm, Speechley Farm and Darlow Farm. Visibility at the time was about 15 yards. A lorry that was carrying three of the injured men together with Dr T. Kuhlo and his medical orderly (both Germans) was in collision with an Eastern Counties bus on the narrow road not far from the scene of the accident. The doctor and the orderly were both badly injured and the bus and the lorry were badly damaged.

The accident happened on a railway crossing with a reputation for narrow escapes, mainly caused by people's negligence in failing to close the gates securely and not being sufficiently observant when crossing the busy main line that carried high-speed traffic to and from London. The crossing lies on a very narrow road and the gates in those days were opened by the road users. The railway company displayed warning notices in prominent positions near the crossing, but people nevertheless were careless and lives were lost.

The tragedy was compounded later that year by an accident that took the life of one of Peterborough's most prominent and well-respected inhabitants, Col A. H. Mellows, who was killed on the same crossing.

On 16 October 1948 the colonel and his friend Mr A. F. Percival were returning home at about 5.25pm after a day's shooting near Conington. The two friends were travelling in the colonel's large black Chrysler car and on reaching Conington level-crossing Colonel Mellows got out of the car and went to the crossing gates and looked up and down the line. The colonel remarked to his friend, 'That's the 4pm to London', but it was his last words. Mr Percival opened the gates and watched the car slowly cross the line. There was a train standing on the south side of the crossing some 200yd away obviously waiting for the signal to proceed northwards towards the crossing. Mr Percival's impression was that Colonel Mellows was looking in one direction at this train and failed to notice the fast express that was bearing down on him from the other direction. The train ploughed into the car and instantly killed the colonel and his dog.

Colonel Mellows was buried with full civic honours and his faithful labrador was buried beside the fatal stretch of line.

In time, there were stories of strange happenings at the crossing. More than twelve signalmen have experienced inexplicable events and some have refused to work the box. Mr D. Ellis, signalman at Conington from 1956 until 1958, remembered looking out from the remote box over the flat wind-swept fens and hearing gates clanging to and fro when they were locked.

In a BBC interview in 1973 several signalmen gave accounts of a large black car that was seen drawing up to the crossing obviously waiting to cross the line. By the time the signalman had walked down to perform his duty, the car had vanished. Other signalmen had experienced the apparition of the phantom car and had heard the crunch of gravel as it approached the crossing. In broad daylight one man was able to define a mascot on the radiator which seemed to be the figure of a lady. Colonel Mellows' car had such a mascot. Everything pointed to the fact that Colonel Mellows had returned to the scene of his tragic death.

Mr Norman Jinks, who had custody of the box for many years, used to take his dog for a walk near the crossing but the animal was always very distressed whenever they passed the spot where Colonel Mellows' labrador was buried.

The whole area was regarded as highly emotive because of the unexplained events; the signal box was later removed as part of the Peterborough area signalling modernisation in the 1970s and the crossing is now controlled by remote-control television from the next box down the line at Holme. Of course the official explanation of the removal of Conington box and the choice of Holme to supervise several crossings in the area will be based on technical considerations but behind the scenes how much of that choice was based on the events at Conington? Some thirty-five years later, the crossing is still regarded with fear at night and few brave people will venture near the scene of two terrible tragedies and the restless spirit of a well-loved member of the local community who seems determined to continue his journey over the busy main line. Today, when high-speed trains fly noisily along the main line over the crossing their passengers little realise that they are passing over the scene of such tragic events.

15

THE UTTERBY HALT MYSTERY

Some seven years ago Mrs Hewitt and her late husband were staying in Louth with friends. Being strangers to the area, one Sunday they decided to go for a ride in their car and explore the local countryside between Louth and Grimsby. They set off on the low road between the marshes from Louth and were heading for home via Fulstow, when they noticed the sign to Ludborough and Louth. Turning into what is locally known as Peartree Lane, they approached the railway crossing at Utterby Halt, over which ran the line from Louth to Grimsby, now used as a freight only line some three times a week. Mr Hewitt remarked to his wife that he thought this was the old Grimsby–Peterborough line that ran through Louth and Boston. Then followed an extraordinary sequence of events.

As soon as the front wheels of the Hewitts' car moved on to the crossing the car stopped. Mr Hewitt sighed and tried without success to restart the engine. An eerie silence descended and in spite of his efforts the car would not start. Mrs Hewitt began to feel very frightened that they might be hit by a train. Before the Hewitts could leave their car a gust of wind hit it, shaking it violently and there was a roaring sound as if a train had gone straight through the vehicle. The combination of wind and the extraordinary sounds terrified the Hewitts who were virtual prisoners in their car. Eventually, an eerie silence returned and Mr Hewitt attempted to restart his car. To his amazement it started instantly and Mr Hewitt moved off the crossing and stopped on the other side.

In a state of severe shock, the Hewitts got out of their car and looked around. The rusty track of the crossing was a bed of tangled weeds. The sturdy gates, paint flaking off the surface, were firmly closed against the railway. Set back a little was the crossing-keeper's cottage with its distinctive Great Northern Railway architecture sturdy as ever. It somewhat reassured the frightened couple who could find nothing unusual to explain their traumatic experience. Deciding to go to the cottage to ask for some possible explanation, Mr Hewitt knocked on the back door to no avail. The place was locked up although there were signs of habitation.

Research by the author to find a possible explanation led to a news item in the Louth *Standard* concerning a ganger called John Edward Lancaster who had the misfortune to step out of the way of a fast-fitted freight train and into the path of the Cleethorpes–London express passenger train. The coroner's report stated that Mr Lancaster had been killed instantly.

Was this the incident that the Hewitts experienced? After all, they had experienced the mighty gusts of wind and the terrifying roar so reminiscent of an express train passing at speed. Certainly the paranormal was at work conjuring up this terrifying event which unnerved the Hewitts. The brief details of Mr Lancaster's fatal accident are as follows:

Fog was laying its dense blanket over the Ludborough area on that damp day in January 1953. It clung to the cutting just south of Ludborough Station and visibility was down to between 6 and 12 yards depending on the terrain. Mr Lancaster was a length ganger and he had just completed his stretch of track and was walking back towards Ludborough on the sleeper ends. The fog man was out at Utterby Halt to warn any train of the level-crossing so the fog detonators would be in position. In these dense foggy conditions Mr Lancaster would have heard the noise of a freight train coming from Louth so he would instinctively step to one side to allow the freight to pass him. Unfortunately the rattling freight train would drown the sound of the Cleethorpes to

London Express hauled by a recently overhauled BI.4–6–0 fresh out of the shops and running very silently and as the driver stated later he didn't see Mr Lancaster until he was almost on top of him so nothing could stop this fatal accident.

So it would appear that this dreadful accident had reoccurred in ghostly fashion, possibly to reassert its violent effect and prompt its memory to survive for eternity. Other points of research have failed to provide any other relevant incidents at Utterby Halt, apart from the story of a lady who was killed by a train in the 1920s when she stepped carelessly from behind a local train from which she had alighted, and the occasion when a broken-down milk float was abandoned on the crossing and was smashed to pieces by a train, the driver escaping injury.

As for logical explanations, they are difficult to find, especially as the forces of the supernatural defy rational explanation. So for the record, the Hewitts' terrifying experience at Utterby Halt refuses to dissipate with the passing years, preferring occasionally to replay the harrowing series of events that cost a man his life.

16

THE HORWICH PHANTOM

Bill Morris, a young apprentice at the L&Y works at Horwich at the beginning of this century, had a strange experience on the works line. This began with an invitation to a footplate ride on a new locomotive's maiden run in recognition of his work.

Horwich works were on a spur of about 4 miles from the main line. One winter's day the foreman asked Bill to join him on the footplate of the cab of a new 0–6–0T. The cab contained inspectors, boilersmiths, the foreman, the duty driver and fireman. Bill was to ride on the footplate and be the look-out when they drove back bunker first.

On the return journey, Bill saw a man walking in the track about 300yd ahead. He was walking towards Horwich and had his back to the engine. Bill shouted to the driver to brake and the driver responded quickly and whistled again. The man ignored the warning signals and walked on. So convinced was the young apprentice that the engine had run over the man and killed him that he stepped down from the engine after it had stopped and walked away. However, before long he heard his name being shouted and then a great deal of laughter. Not only was there no sign of a body beneath the train, but also no mark of footprints in the snow.

'Would you mind telling us how your friend can walk along the sleeper in 4in of snow without leaving a single footprint?' they asked sarcastically.

From that moment, Bill was the object of ridicule both at

the works and in his social life. Before long, the story of Bill and the ghostly figure on the railway track spread around the town and the young man was unable to tolerate the jeering to which he was subjected. He left home and found work at BMC, Cowley.

Almost a year later he returned home and happened to relate his strange experience to a publican. He had hardly finished the story when the publican asked his wife to fetch an old leather-bound book which contained the tale of a man seen walking along the works line at Horwich in thick snow and who had been oblivious to a train's warning signal. That was fifty years to the day that Bill himself had seen the apparition.

17

IN AND AROUND LONDON

Lewisham

A few years ago, a British Rail bridge inspector, who worked on the St John's flyover, was waiting for a bus at about 2am at Lewisham clock tower, some 100yd from Lewisham Southern Railway station. While he was waiting, he heard someone calling for help. The voice seemed to be coming from the roof of the tall buildings around him and the person appeared to be trapped. The inspector telephoned the police and a patrol car soon arrived. The policeman, who also heard the voice, was not perturbed, however.

'No one is trapped there,' he reassured the inspector. 'People often hear voices calling for help. They are the people who were killed in the Lewisham, St John's, train disaster in December 1957 and it is a well-known fact here that the phenomenon has been active since the crash.'

Moorgate

During the winter of 1974–5 workmen employed on adapting the Great Northern and City Tube tunnels for main line working often saw a man dressed in blue overalls walking towards them in the tunnel at night. As he approached they were terrified to see that his face bore a look of indescribable horror; he then vanished into the tunnel wall. It is believed that it was the ghost of a maintenance worker who was killed by a train on that stretch of line.

After the Moorgate disaster of February 1975, some news-papers reported that the apparition may have caused the driver's lapse of concentration which caused the crash. On the other hand, the ghost may have been a premonition of the disaster.

Highgate High Level

This station, situated in a deep cutting with tunnels at each end, possesses an eerie atmosphere. During the early years of this century, a man is said to have walked into one of the tunnels in the path of an approaching train to commit suicide and his ghost is reputed to haunt the place.

The station was completely rebuilt in 1941 for the Northern Line extension from Finsbury Park to Alexandra Palace–East Finchley. The work was never completed, however, and the extension was abandoned. The line was closed to passenger traffic in July 1954 and to British Rail freight in 1964, and was finally lifted in 1971 after six years' use to tow empty Tube trains to and from the Northern City line.

The modern station buildings stand forlornly in the deserted cutting without tracks and almost hidden by foliage, giving an emotive, eerie atmosphere. People who have stood on the station have experienced the feeling that they were being watched and others living near the closed line at Highgate and Crouch End claim they have heard sounds of trains at night.

Alexandra Palace

When Alexandra Palace was built in the 1860s, gypsies had an encampment on the hill-top where the building was located. They were evicted by the builders and subsequently put a curse on the building with the words: 'May death and destruc-tion befall this place and everything associated with it.'

Within a year of its opening, Alexandra Palace was burnt down. Although it was subsequently rebuilt, for most of its existence it was regarded as a 'white elephant' and when plans were coming to fruition concerning its revival the palace was burnt down again in 1980. Two railway lines were laid to serve the place: that to Palace Gates closed in 1963, while that to the palace itself closed in 1954 after it was so nearly linked to the Northern City Tube into Moorgate. Thus, both were doomed to failure.

Could the gypsies' wrath have been responsible for the non-completion of the Northern Line's extension, and even for the Moorgate Tube disaster? Ironically, plans have recently been approved for a multi-million pound scheme to rebuild the palace into a major leisure complex. One can only surmise at any future disasters.

18

DALGARVEN SIGNAL BOX

Signal boxes are emotive places and are often the locations for the paranormal. Perhaps because of their remote and lonely situations they become the ideal setting for ghostly phenomena.

The late Derek Cross, the well-known railway photographer and raconteur, discovered such a story concerning Dalgarven box situated between Dalry and Kilwinning on the old G&SW main line. Although an intermediate blockpost, it nevertheless played an important role. There were no loops or cross-overs, but it was still practical to maintain the safe running of the line. The box was at the end of a farm track and was extremely primitive, having no light or water so that signalmen would have had to cross all four main lines and trudge down a muddy farm track to the outside tap for water.

The original experience happened in the middle of World War I. The night-shift worker, on taking over the shift, would go to the farm to replenish his water supply. The high density of wartime traffic was such that crossing the line at any time was dangerous. On one occasion, unknown to the signalman who was crossing the line, a goods train had been let away from Kilwinning on the up-Glasgow slow line and consequently he was killed. As it was during the war, no significant inquiries were made, but the suspicion lingers that the signalman at Kilwinning let the goods train out of his loop without putting it on the block. However, such were the strange happenings at Dalgarven box that nobody would work the box at night.

Mr Cross visited the site several times towards the end of the age of steam, when it was worked only on morning shifts, as he was interested in the stories of the ghost. It was a relief man's job as nobody would take it regularly and locals would not visit the box even in daylight. On one occasion, the relief worker asked Mr Cross if he had come to photograph the ghost. Another signalman said that he had seen the ghost on summer nights and although it was harmless he did not enjoy the experience of the apparition.

A legend grew up that the ghost was seen only before an accident and, following a crash at Dalry in the late 1940s, the signalman at Dalgarven swore that his attention had been distracted by a man walking across the track. The inquiry proved that nobody had walked across the track at the time in question, so the cause of the accident remained a mystery. Dalgarven has gone now and it is difficult to even see where it was situated, but the story of the ghostly signalman will remain forever.

19

THE MYSTERIOUS ATMOSPHERE
AT SHANKEND

Some places are shrouded in an aura of dread or horror which
defies any rational explanation, thus deterring researchers and
those who would try to probe its secrets. Such a place is
Shankend with its lonely derelict mansion and large weed-
infested garden. In its heyday the mansion was an imposing
house overlooking the scenic Waverley line as it followed the
undulating Border countryside, the remoteness of its situation
allowing superb views of the winding railway.

The late Derek Cross visited the mansion in 1951 as it was
ideally situated to photograph the line. Knowing nothing
about the place and its past, he decided to explore the terrain to
find a spot to set up his camera. However, he experienced
such a strong sense of evil in the place, even in the summer
sunshine, that he was forced to pack up his equipment and
leave.

Some time later he mentioned his experience to the late
Bishop Eric Treacy, the doyen of railway photography. To
Derek Cross' surprise, the bishop stated that the place reeked
of evil and he would never return there.

A school-friend of Mr Cross, a keen hill-walker, mentioned
that a superb photograph could be taken on the hill above
Shankend. When Derek Cross replied that he knew of the spot
but would not wish to return to the place, his friend said that
he had felt the same sense of evil. His dog, a bold bull terrier, had

also become terrified when he was in the location.

Some years later, Mr Cross was talking to a friend who specialised in sound recordings of railways and mentioned Shankend. The friend replied that he had made only one visit and he would never return.

Such was the consistency of people's experience at Shankend that Derek Cross decided to investigate the mystery. Apparently, during World War I the mansion and its grounds were taken over as a prison camp for German prisoners-of-war. Following an outbreak of typhoid or cholera, in which many of the prisoners died, the bodies were buried more or less where they fell. After the end of the war, the estate was sold, but nobody stayed long and it finally fell into disrepair. When Mr Cross asked the locals to show him around the place, not one was prepared to venture near the site, even on a fine day. Such is the feeling of impending doom at Shankend that one's only desire is to leave the place and never return.

20

THE GREY TRAIN

The Highlands of Scotland have always been known for their beauty and scenic grandeur, and their attraction to tourists from all over the world is understandable. The average tourist, however, does not see or experience the mysteries and vestiges of the past that reoccur to the residents of the tiny Scottish villages and hamlets. John MacDonald has lived in the Highlands for all of his seventy-eight years and he has a story to relate that defies belief.

The year was 1921 and it was on the last day of the year. I had been playing my melodion at a concert at the Dunphail school which was situated next to the railway line which was the old Highland Railway. The school was about a mile south of Dunphail Station. I was making my way home, walking on the track side (I knew that I was safe because the last train had long gone that night). It was in the early hours just after midnight on a beautiful moonlight night and although I had enjoyed myself that evening I was sober and happy. So I was singing and whistling without a care in the world. I had just got through the rocky chasm near the junction where the Perth line curves away to the south and a hundred-mile journey, but where I was at the moment many strange things have been seen during the hours of darkness on the railway line.

This particular area between Dava and Dunphail seems to have a very mysterious aura about it and the local folk cannot explain their fear, but never take a chance ere some harm would befall them. Anyway, at this moment I felt a strange feeling of fear and the hairs on the back of my neck started to rise and I had a feeling that there was a train on the line. Now there shouldn't have been. The service trains had finished and unless the Highland Railway had reason to send a special train at this hour remains a puzzle. I felt this fear very strong and I felt compelled to turn and look back along the line and to my horror there was a train coming full pelt towards me. Clouds of smoke pouring out of its chimney, hauling four brightly lit carriages but with nobody in them. Also nobody was on the footplate but the glow of the fire lit the controls up very clearly. I quickly scrambled up the embankment to get out of the way. Then I noticed that the train did not seem to be making contact with the track. It appeared to be about 2ft or so above the rails, almost floating. It was very eerie and ethereal and I was dumbfounded, almost unable to believe what I had seen before my eyes. I felt a feeling of terror overcome me as I watched the ghostly train float out of sight in a swirl of mist. I sat on the bank side unable to collect my thoughts. What had I witnessed? At last I was able to make my way home. I didn't tell anyone of what I had seen. I was too scared to talk to even my friends at that time.

But forty years later when I was married and living here with my wife and family I set out one lovely summer morning on my bicycle to go to Dunphail to see my mother who was living alone in Bogney Farm House where I was born (my father had passed on some fifteen years before) and my mother wouldn't leave the old family home. I was pleased to find her fairly well but she told me that her sister, Mrs Robertson who lived at Carnoch near Dunphail Station, had been very poorly, so one night my mother set out to walk down the railway line to visit her. About 11 o'clock mother set off for home and when she was coming up the line about a mile from Bogney she had a terrible fright. She thought she heard a train coming up the line but she knew that there couldn't be a train at that time of night. But she felt compelled to look back over her shoulder, and sure enough there was the grey train coming up full steam ahead. She hurriedly climbed up the bank and sat down. She then witnessed with terror the phantom train in its awesome fullness — the smoke pouring out of the chimney, the empty deserted footplate, the fierce glow of the fire, and the brightly lit but empty carriages, all possibly 2ft above the track. She agreed with me that it seemed to float. She was terrified and for a time could not move. After a while she was able to resume her journey home and lay down on the couch with her clothes still on such was the shock to her nerves. It was daylight when she came to and she was able to go to the door and look out over the line. Everything was calm and still. She looked at the clock. It was midday and she hurried to the door to wave to the driver of the midday train as it passed. The driver waved back and threw out a newspaper for her which he always did and her little dog then ran to the railway and brought back the paper.

Mother was astonished when I told her that I had witnessed the grey train many years before. We talked about it in detail for hours wondering what it could mean and we were both convinced that something was going to happen on that line. [As if their thoughts were answered, an accident occurred soon after when a track foreman was run down and killed by a train.]

Now there is no railway. The track and almost every visible sign of a railway has gone, probably forever, leaving the ghost or ghosts to indulge themselves without interference. But things were not finished yet because my sister Mary was to experience the strange happenings on that stretch of line, but in a slightly different way. She was walking home on the line years after mother had her fright and again Mary was near Dunphail Station when she had a strange feeling that something was going to happen, and it did. Some unknown force hit her in the back hurling her to the ground. She was unable to get up for some time but she managed to crawl home in a very bad way. She was never the same jolly girl again. She was 16 years old then and she lived another twenty years but was not the same and not happily, so the experience was to have its lasting effect on the people that were chosen to see it.

21

THE MYSTERIOUS ENCOUNTER
AT PINMORE

In June 1966 the late Derek Cross decided to photograph the Paddy — the nickname of the Euston to Stranraer express — at Pinmore. It had been a year since the old Port Road to Stranraer line had closed and the London to Stranraer trains were diverted via Ayr and Girvan. The removal of the box at Pinmore made his photograph possible as it gave an unimpeded view of the subject.

Mr Cross had chosen the ideal spot for his photography some three days earlier and the picture he wanted could only be taken during the ten days around the longest day when the sun came through a gap in the hills.

To explain the nature of the Stranraer line, the initial grade up to the Pinmore tunnel is 1 in 54 and runs for about 4 miles. The tunnel cuts through a saddle into the valley of the Stinchar river, so on a calm morning even a heavy train on the bank could hardly be heard from the Pinmore side of the tunnel. The summit of this very steep grade was in the tunnel and once out of it engines would shut off to get their breath back.

The train was due to pass through Pinmore at 5am. Mr Cross walked to the signal box at Girvan and waited until the train was belled off Kilkerran which gave him sufficient time to drive to Pinmore. That particular morning, which was midsummer's eve, the train was 20 minutes late. Mr Cross drove to the tiny village of Pinmore, parked his car in the old

57

goods yard of the deserted station and made his way towards the line. Suddenly, a girl aged about 16 walked up from one of the scattered houses in the village and stood in the same spot he intended to use for his photography. He wished the girl good morning and mentioned that he intended to photograph the Paddy. To his surprise, she did not reply but looked at him so vaguely that he inferred that she had not heard him.

In due course, Mr Cross took the photograph he had come for and the girl crossed the narrow road and watched the train drop down into the valley. Although Mr Cross was perturbed at his strange encounter, he dismissed his consternation and decided that she must have been a village girl who had watched the train and then returned home.

On reflection, however, he became increasingly puzzled by the mysterious young lady. *He* had known that the train was running late, but how could *she* have known it? Yet she had timed her appearance so exactly that it seemed as if she had been forewarned of the train's arrival. Even if she had heard the locomotive's whistle as it entered the tunnel, she would not have had time to run to the bridge in time to meet Mr Cross as he parked his car in the goods yard.

Derek Cross intended to photograph the Glasgow to Stranraer goods train that followed the Paddy, but he felt so uneasy that he drove straight back to Girvan. He explained his reason for returning so hurriedly to the crew of the Stranraer goods train. The late Jimmy Irvine, one of the drivers, said, 'Och, ye've seen that lassie that threw herself under a train at Pinmore in 1939.'

Some time later, Derek Cross learned more details about the tragic death of the girl. Shortly before the war, she had committed suicide by throwing herself from the bridge into the path of a train. In 1939 fashions were similar to the 1960s vogue, which may explain why Mr Cross believed the girl was real rather than an apparition. He was left with the distinct feeling that he had encountered someone from the spirit world on that early midsummer's morning.

22

STRANGE SOUNDS ON THE
WAVERLEY ROUTE

In April 1961, when making recordings on the Carlisle–
Edinburgh 'Waverley' route that has made a niche in the hearts
of so many railway enthusiasts, Peter Handford had spent the
day on Whitrope summit, but had eventually abandoned attempts at recording because of the unfavourable direction of
the wind. He decided to move down to Stobs to attempt
recordings on the other side of Whitrope summit on the climb
from Hawick.

It was nearly dark when he arrived at Stobs and set up his
equipment in a previously selected position above a deep cutting on the Whitrope side of the station. By the time the first
train had climbed up from Hawick through the station into the
cutting and away towards Shankend, it was pitch dark. Mr
Handford was disappointed with the recording as the sounds
did not meet his expectations, but by then it was too dark and
too late to make a change of location. Another train came by,
but again the recording was unsatisfactory. It was by now only
an hour or two before midnight. Another train was due and,
listening through headphones, he was puzzled by inexplicably
eerie sounds which seemed to come from a group of trees
nearby, above the cutting. He switched on the recorder briefly
to record any distant sounds which would add atmosphere to
those of the approaching train and the distant whistle of the engine. All Mr Handford heard, however, were the eerie sounds

which seemed to be a faint moaning and chuckling coming from the nearby wood. The expected train eventually arrived, but just as it approached, one channel of the recorder inexplicably failed, ruining the recording. For the next hour or two, Mr Handford tried to rectify the fault in the chilly darkness, but as it proved impossible, he decided to wait until daylight and to get some sleep meanwhile.

In the morning, having rectified the recorder fault, he walked down towards the station to look for a new location. He decided that on the way he would take a look at the nearby clump of trees from which the eerie sounds had drifted during the night. There was no sign of animal habitation, no sheep in the area, no birds' nests or birds to be seen in the trees. Having walked among the trees, he noticed a group of metal markers protruding from the ground recording the names of German soldiers who were buried there after their deaths in a prisoner-of-war camp that was established in the area during World War I.

In subsequent night-recording sessions, of which there were several on the Waverley route, Peter Handford always took care to use a location in a clearing in the woods above Stobs Station rather than return to that first location above the cutting.

23

THE DISAPPEARING PASSENGER
AT KIRKHILL

When dealing with the paranormal or supernatural, it is easy to look for rational explanations, but logical reasoning cannot always explain the strange events that occur in people's lives. James Tomlinson had a mysterious experience which defied rational explanation and he is resigned to the fact that he will never satisfactorily solve the enigma of the disappearing passenger.

Mr Tomlinson was a guard on an EMU on the electric railway system in the Glasgow area and the incident occurred in the mid-1970s. On about the last trip of the night-shift, around dawn, the EMU on which he was working was approaching Kirkhill, the terminal of that particular service. On arrival at the station, Mr Tomlinson saw a man about 5½ft tall wearing a dark coat and a soft trilby hat. He was carrying a briefcase and was walking along the cross-over on to the platform. As the train halted, the man was standing on the platform, obviously waiting to board the train for the return journey. When Mr Tomlinson had changed the train indicator board on the EMU for its return journey, he turned to look down the platform. The passenger was nowhere to be seen. Mr Tomlinson became very anxious and looked for the passenger both on and under the train. He had completely disappeared. The driver had not seen anyone on the platform and neither had the booking office clerk. So the mystery remained: where had the man gone?

James Tomlinson could not and still does not believe that he imagined seeing the mysterious passenger. Although he was subjected to ridicule by his colleagues, he remained firmly convinced. His only explanation is that possibly the gentleman had travelled on the line for many years in the past and that his ghost fitted into a well-worn slot in time. So was the ghostly passenger preparing to embark on another train journey as he had done many times during his life on earth? We shall never know, and James Tomlinson remains mystified by his unique experience.

24

A TRICK OF THE LIGHT

The following story concerns the sighting of a Deltic seen clearly entering Hadley Wood South tunnel, bearing the number 55020 *Nimbus*, even though the locomotive had been cut up seven months previously. The story was written by an observer and appeared in the *Deltic Deadline,* issue No 17.

When the day's main force has been spent, and the sun is sinking slowly beyond Penzance, the twilight comes to the confines of Hadley Woods. That strange zone of time and light between day and night is broken only by bats wheeling and diving across the expanse of the East Coast main line. Somewhere a dog howls. An up local slows to a halt at the signals on the edge of the woods. Everything seems as it should be. The moon is beginning to take the twilight, temperature drops alarmingly, there's a real chill in the air. In the distance comes the familiar note of a Deltic engine but there's nothing scheduled. It's a bonus for the late train spotter. Out from the New Barnet footbridge comes the Deltic, the throb of the Napier engines very reassuring, it seems. However, somehow different, somehow surrounded by a glow, an aura, perhaps a trick of the light.

While the local train gets the road and moves off, the Deltic moves on, again the familiar engines making the exhaust stand up into the dusk sky. Nothing can be wrong, surely? As it passes I turn and watch it enter Hadley Wood South tunnel. I shout to my friend, 'Did you get the number?'

'55020' comes the reply. 'Yes, that's what I thought'. For a few silent moments this doesn't click into place. Then, we suddenly realise what we've said. But, *Nimbus* was cut up seven months ago.

At Hadley Wood Station we are told that no southbound train has passed through. A trick of the light?

One can understand a steam locomotive appearing wreathed in smoke and surplus steam to fascinate the unsuspecting person and seemingly so solid that one could reach out and touch it, but a Deltic? Here is a new dimension of the paranormal, the sound of a diesel motor coming from a train that appeared long after it had been scrapped.

It should be remembered that Hadley Wood tunnel and the East Coast main line was a favourite haunt of the Deltics that used it for almost all of their working life, so it is not surprising that one of their number should reappear on its familiar route. For the record, No 55020 *Nimbus* was taken into service on 2 December 1962 and named the same day. It was withdrawn on 18 December 1979 and was cut up at Doncaster on 2 February 1980.

25

MYSTERIOUS NOISES AT
WINSOR HILL TUNNEL

In the early summer of 1956, Peter Handford was in the process of preparing to record traffic on the now defunct Somerset & Dorset line. He went first to Winsor Hill tunnel, situated in a lonely spot approached by a climb over a viaduct from Shepton Mallet. The chosen location was on the Shepton Mallet side of the tunnel, where he intended to record trains approaching the climb. The tunnel, a short one, was a single bore as the up and down lines were separated there.

As always, when deciding on recording locations, Mr Handford reconnoitred the surrounding area. On the far side of the tunnel, near the side of the line towards Bath, there was an immensely deep rock quarry, disused and deserted but containing some old equipment, rusting away at the bottom. The whole area had a horribly uneasy and melancholy atmosphere and he noticed that from time to time on that bright summer's day occasional metallic rattlings came from the depths of the quarry. The sounds were inexplicable since the wind was blowing from the Glastonbury direction and the high ground shielded the quarry from it, as shown by the fact that the stunted bushes on the lip of the quarry did not move.

The strange metallic noises continued at intervals, whenever he was in a position to hear them. Although Peter Handford had intended to return to the Bath side of the tunnel at night to make recordings of the several trains which at that time ran from the north towards Bournemouth in the early hours of Saturday morning, he did not do so, partly because he was reluctant to visit the place in darkness and also because each time he visited Winsor Hill tunnel to make recordings he experienced problems and misfortunes of one sort or another.

On the first occasion a violent thunderstorm blew up on that beautiful summer day, wrecking any attempt at further recording and causing damage to the equipment. On other occasions a wind suddenly blew from a direction which made recording trains on the climb from Shepton Mallet impossible, or a sudden rain storm blew up at an inopportune moment. Worst of all, perhaps, on a day of perfect weather conditions, the recording equipment suffered an inexplicable fault which was impossible to rectify on location so that the whole trip was wasted.

Years later, when Peter Handford had met the late Derek Cross, they discussed the Somerset & Dorset line. Quite un-prompted, Mr Cross related his experience of the place which tallied precisely with Peter Handford's, especially with regard to the disused quarry on the Bath side of Winsor Hill tunnel.

26

THE GHOST OF DARLINGTON
NORTH ROAD STATION

The following story was published in the Darlington and
Stockton Times *on 9 January 1960.*

More than a century ago the nightwatchman at North Road
Station had a ghastly experience. This was before the North
Road bridge was built, and the Stockton and Darlington
Railway line passed over the Great North Road by a level-
crossing. Mr James Durham, the nightwatchman, had a
cabin near the crossing and his beat was from the old goods
station, east of the crossing to the passenger station on the
west. One winter's night about midnight, after his first
perambulations, Durham went to the porter's cellar at the
station to have supper. The cellar had been originally part of
a railwayman's house and was provided with a fireplace and
a gas jet and the room gave access to a coal cellar.

Descending the stone steps from the station platform,
Durham turned up the gas and had just sat down on the
bench and opened his bait tin when he was startled by the
apparition of a strange man followed by a large black
retriever dog emerging from the coal cellar.

Realising that his visitor was no ordinary mortal, the
watchman did not challenge him but jumping to his feet he
kept his eyes fixed firmly on the intruder, hoping thereby to
induce him to retire. He noticed that the ghost was smartly

dressed in a cut-away coat with gilt buttons, a stand-up collar and Scotch cap.

Walking towards the fire the ghost raised his hand and struck the watchman a smart blow on the body which produced a strange sensation. Mustering all the courage he possessed the watchman assumed a defiant attitude and dealt the ghost a straight right blow to the body.

Durham's hand went right through the apparition and struck the fireplace, bruising his knuckles. The ghost shrieked out and fell backwards to the wall, whereupon the dog rushed forward and seized Durham's leg. Although as he explained afterwards, Durham experienced a sense of pain, an examination of the skin revealed no mark or puncture of the skin. The ghost, having regained its upright position, called the dog by a click of his tongue and the intruders retreated into the coal cellar.

Taking his lantern the watchman followed and although there was no other entrance but from the porter's room, he could find no trace of his antagonists.

The railway ghost caused a great stir in Darlington at the time but many were very sceptical about its bona fides. The excitement was intensified when it became known that some time previously a railway clerk named Winter, who kept a black retriever, had shot himself in the porter's cellar but Durham had claimed that he was unaware of the tragedy when he had encountered the ghost.

Many people questioned the watchman to his condition on the night of the incident. One of them was Edward Pease, who invited Durham to his home and asked him many questions. Had he been asleep at the time? Was he subject to nightmares? Had he been drinking? Durham maintained that he was a teetotaller, his mind was free of trouble at that time, and that he had all his faculties.

The Rev Henry Kendal, Minister of Union Street Congregational Church from 1859-1893 testified to Durham's straightforwardness. Durham was a regular attender at Mr Kendal's church and he was regarded as a strong reliable man whose word could be trusted.

Sometime after, the Society for Psychical Research was founded in 1882 and Mr Kendal sent details of the North Road Station incident to the President, Prof Sidgwick, who asked for further details of Durham's bodily state on the eventful night. It was pointed out that he was a regular watchman who slept during the day so as to be able to perform his nightly duties. He had only been in the cellar for about one minute when the ghost appeared and he had had no time to doze.

In 1891 the Society conducted a 'Census of Hallucinations' throughout the country and Mr W. T. Stead, the journalist, assisted by enclosing some 100,000 census papers in the *Review of Reviews* which he edited. This magazine published the story of the Darlington railway ghost as one of the most thrilling of a series of ghostly anecdotes.

Mr Kendal inspected the cellar in 1891 and found the place exactly as it had been when Durham used it. A few days ago I went warily — in broad daylight — down the steps to examine the cellar. The whole room, part of larger premises, is now used for coal storage but the salient features of the story, the fireplace and coal recess are in situ and it was not difficult to reconstruct the strange winter scene of over four generations ago.

A James Durham died on January 7th 1917 aged 75 and I recently stood by his grave in the North Cemetery. The ghost fighter has now reached that blessed state: 'Where the wicked cease from troubling and the weary are at rest.'

27

THE BOY AT ENTWHISTLE HALT

D. K. McKenzie remembers a chilling story told by his uncle, Tom Ackroyd, who, from the time he left school in 1925, worked for the railway.

In 1935 Ackroyd was put in charge of Entwhistle Halt on the Darwen–Bolton line. There was nothing special about the halt: it had a signal cabin, about a dozen levers, and a pair of gates to allow carts to cross to the farms scattered across the moors. Apart from the occasional passenger, the main traffic was milk churns en route to the dairy and dye wagons from Preston. The sidings were situated about half a mile away and there was a water-tower nearby. Ackroyd enjoyed a quiet bachelor life and lived in a small house by the crossing.

Ackroyd's strange experience began one day as he looked out from his lonely signal box. He knew most of the men who used the line and passed the time of day with them. However, there was one person he saw frequently yet never spoke to him, nor even knew his name. He first noticed a young boy early one summer, about a year or so after he had taken over Entwhistle Halt. One Saturday at about 3 o'clock when the 2.47 had not long gone through and he had put the 'line clear' through, he was standing at the window and saw the lad. He was no more than eight or nine, playing in the meadow on the far side of the up line to Darwen. He was running, just as children of that age do, almost as if he was chasing the shadows across the moor. At first, Ackroyd thought nothing about it,

70

but he saw him again the following Saturday at about the same time.

All through the summer he ran about in the meadow, chasing the shadows. The sheep were obviously used to him, for they never moved much for him. He came so often afterwards that Ackroyd began to look out for him when Saturday came round. He was a thin lad, dressed in dark short trousers and a grey pullover. Although he did not appear to be undernourished, he was pale-faced. After a while, Ackroyd thought that he belonged to one of the local farms, and that because of his pale complexion he was recovering from an illness. The young boy did not appear after about September, but as the winters were so severe on the moors Ackroyd was not surprised.

During the summer months of the war years, Ackroyd watched the boy playing in the meadow beside the line. Towards the end of spring, he saw him earlier than usual, and he saw him several times standing close beside the crossing gates on the up side, his face almost pressing between the bars. In an inexplicable way, the lad looked a pathetic sight. His little pale face always looked pinched and very sad. He stood at the gates evening after evening, but was always gone when the 5.13 to Blackburn went through.

One Saturday, late in June, in the last year of the war, Ackroyd had passed the 5.13 through as usual and received the 5.29 from Chorley and seen it in. Normally, he let it through at 5.43, except that on that particular Saturday he received it a minute or so late. It was 5.33 when he rang through the 'train in section' and 5.48 when he put the signal to green and heard the train start up. Suddenly, however, he heard a lot of confused noises — the brakes screeched, steam hissed, and people were screaming and shouting. Ackroyd put the signals to red, rang the station down the line to tell them that he had a problem and then rang the next station above to alert them that he still had a train in his section. He then alerted the down line either side of him. All this he did before he even knew what had happened. When he had time to take account of the situation, it seemed that Bill Oldenshaw had fallen under the train at the crossing and been killed outright. The driver had not even seen him.

At about 8 o'clock there was a knock on Ackroyd's door. He opened it and found the line foreman standing on his doorstep.

'Now, then, Tom Ackroyd,' he said.

'Ow do,' replied the signalman.

'It's a bad business is this, Tom,' he said. 'That were Bill Oldenshaw, him as has the farm over by Stones Place. That's the second from the family that's gone same way.'

'Nay,' said Ackroyd. 'I've been here some time now and it's never happened before.'

'No, well,' said the foreman. 'That last one were a long time before your time, Tom. I reckon it were about the time of the Great War. It were Bill's older brother. Bill were not more than a baby when his brother Harold died. Oh aye, I remember hearing that tale when I first joined. I were no more than a lad myself. Harold was about eight or nine and he was always playing and running about in that meadow yonder.'

Ackroyd knew immediately where he meant and his blood ran cold as he knew what the foreman was going to say next.

'Aye, he used to look out for his dad's cart on a Saturday at about 4.45 and he'd wait for it to come across the line there. Anyway, this Saturday he was late, no one knew why, and Harold just stood with his face against there waiting. Then he must have seen his father and the cart because the next thing anyone knew, he was through that gate and across — and that's when he went right under the 5.29.'

28

THE APPLEBY HALL OAK CHEST

Some years ago, when the locomotive shed was closed at Keadby and engine power was concentrated at Frodingham, a pump-house was built beside the line to supply water to the new Frodingham locomotive depot. This pump-house was fully automatic and the latest example of technological design. It required servicing approximately once a month and usually three electricians from Scunthorpe carried out the work. The most convenient time for this routine servicing was on a Sunday and the three men soon became familiar with the sophisticated equipment.

One Sunday, when the three men had finished their lunch break, they decided to walk across the scrubland which was adjacent to the main railway line. The weather was fine and they were enjoying their walk when they came across the neglected remains of a large house which they had often seen in the distance from the pump-house. After viewing the outside and the wild, overgrown garden, they decided to explore the crumbling interior. It was a sad sight with the faded grandeur of a once noble family home. The interior had been vandalised and parts of the house were obviously unsafe. The men moved about cautiously, looking with curiosity at what they might find. Suddenly, under a pile of wood, rubble and plaster, they found an old wooden box in remarkably good condition. After examining it, they considered it would make a good tool-box and decided to take it with them.

On examining their find more closely at the pump-house,

they found that the box was of stout construction and very old. The inside of the lid bore a faint inscription which the men could not read. They decided to leave the box in the pump house until their next visit. Suddenly, however, strange events took place. Inexplicably, the usually reliable pumps started to malfunction and finally broke down. And one of the electricians, a seemingly healthy man, was suddenly taken ill and rushed to hospital with a suspected heart attack.

One of the men then read an article in the *Grimsby Evening Telegraph* about Appleby Hall. Apparently, an old oak chest had been part of the family's possessions for generations and bore an inscription inside the lid which said in effect, 'Whoever removes this chest from Appleby Hall, ill luck will befall them.' Realising the cause of the inexplicable events that had recently occurred, the electrician telephoned the police. Subsequently, the box was collected from the pump-house and returned to Appleby Hall where it was returned to its place among the ruins.

As if by retribution, the sick electrician made a remarkable recovery and the pumps resumed their efficient, reliable operation. The strange experiences no doubt left an indelible mark on the memories of the three electricians who would never forget the malevolent power of that old wooden box.

29

'HUMPHREY' OF NORMANBY PARK

Normanby Park steel works and rolling mills were, in their heyday, one of the most viable processors of steel in the world and provided employment for thousands of people in and around the Scunthorpe area. Like any vast industrial complex, it had its own substantial railway sidings to move and accept train loads of iron ore and to ship the completed products en route to its customers worldwide. However, despite its firm footing in the industrial world, the works had a frequent visitor from another plane, a ghostly figure known as 'Humphrey'.

It was believed that Humphrey was a farm worker employed on the Normanby Park estate in the distant past and that he had been found guilty of stealing from his employers. Apparently, he was beaten to death and, as a result, swore that he would forever haunt the local area. If the legend is true, he kept his word for he was seen on countless occasions over the years. In the shape of a little old man, bent and stooping, with an old bag on his shoulder, he appeared and disappeared at whim, often through walls and machinery, and terrifying anyone who saw him. He frightened train crews who saw him walking aimlessly on the railway tracks as if he were a real person.

One night, a works policeman was disturbed in his office by a tramp-like figure wearing a strange hat. The policeman turned and spoke to the man and asked him what he wanted. However, the intruder refused to reply and disappeared through a wall. This incident so affected the policeman that he suffered a nervous breakdown from which, it is said, he never fully recovered.

Much to the consternation of the operators, Humphrey's shabby figure would appear and then disappear into high-speed machinery. One young man, who was attending a large machine which was railed off as a safety precaution, warned Humphrey of the dangers of moving machinery. The ghost, however, paid no heed, walked through the machinery and disappeared through a wall.

It seems that Humphrey had several favourite places where he viewed the progress of the works, one such place being between the weighbridge and the steel works. One of the works engine drivers had a traumatic experience when he saw the old tramp pass straight through the train of works wagons as he was moving them. The shocked driver assumed that he had run over and killed someone on the line, but on investigation there was no injured person to be found.

About twenty years ago, after dusk, a weighbridge office employee reported seeing a tramp-like figure walk into the weighbridge office, look around, and then walk through the back wall of the office.

Humphrey did not confine his activities solely to the steel works and walked across the fields he had known during his earthly days. One old lady recalls her days as a midwife many years ago when on one occasion she had to deliver a baby in an old farm cottage near the works. As she prepared to mount her bicycle to return home after the delivery, the proud father called out, 'If you see Humphrey, don't be frightened, he is quite harmless.' When she learned who Humphrey was, she only visited the cottage in daylight.

An unnerving experience was witnessed by the train crew of a Class 31 diesel locomotive that was leaving Normanby Park sidings with a train of empty iron-ore hoppers, en route to Immingham docks. As the train approached the main line, from the sidings, the locomotive's second man drew the driver's attention to the shadowy figure of a tramp walking along the line in front of them. The driver braked hard and sounded the whistle, but the man ignored the warning and disappeared under the train. Fearing the worst, the driver and second man got off the locomotive and examined the train and the line side, but could find nothing untoward. When the guard learned what had happened, he simply laughed and said that it must have been old Humphrey.

30

THE ELSHAM PHANTOM TRAIN

Rumours of a ghostly train that appeared in foggy conditions near Ancholme Bridge on the line between Elsham and Worlaby led Ted Smith and Jack Brookes, two reliable men in their mid-fifties, to investigate the tales and discover the truth for themselves. Both men were sceptical about ghosts and the supernatural and their jaunt in suitably foggy conditions was aimed at returning to their friends who believed the stories and good-humouredly disprove them. Not for one moment did the two men believe that they would see anything, and they were determined not to allow the foggy weather to play havoc with their imaginations.

As the light of that winter day faded and the swirling fog closed in, the two friends took shelter in a platelayer's cabin at the northern end of the line's long curve. Before long, their confidence changed to an icy fear as they discerned through the enveloping fog the shape of a railway engine lit up by an eerie glowing aura. They were able to make out the locomotive's smoke-box and cab, and the glare of the fire reflecting through the spectacle plate on the cab front. Knowing that it was a basic railway practice to use detonators in foggy conditions to protect signals, etc, and as the sound they emitted carried some distance, the men awaited the series of bangs that would herald the presence of a train. Whatever this strange apparition was that held them in its awe, reality would return when the bangs announced a train that belonged to this world.

'It's a bit strange, isn't it?' asked Jack.

Ted nodded. 'Doesn't look right to me, and it doesn't seem to be getting any nearer.'

'Surely the fog signals are out,' said Jack. 'Hope it's not that ghost train they keep talking about.'

Both men laughed nervously, neither sure of the truth.

'Tell you what,' said Ted. 'Let's go and see if we can see the fogs, then when we're sure about them, perhaps we can get a close look at the engine — perhaps it's broken down.'

Jack agreed and they set off down the track side, treading carefully in case they tripped over signal wire.

Reassuring themselves that the train had broken down, both men felt confident that they would find nothing untoward on the line. Soon, however, they found themselves in a nightmare situation for although they were walking towards the train they seemed to get no nearer to it. They could see the train, but it seemed to be in a haze or a glowing flame. The two men continued walking, trying to fathom the mystery of the fog-bound train.

'Just a minute, Ted,' said Jack. 'There's something strange going on and we're not getting any nearer, and look, there's some fog detectors clamped on the rail.'

Ted frowned and shivered. The fog was getting acrid now. Both men cleared their throats. The haze still surrounded the distant locomotive and train, discernible but somehow blurred.

'Come on, Jack, let's go home. I don't like this at all.'

Jack readily agreed. He was feeling the clammy cold that seemed to penetrate his thick coat and chill his bones. The two men groped their way back to the cabin, occasionally glancing back to see what had happened to the strange engine.

Nearing the platelayer's cabin, they both stopped and looked back. They could not believe their eyes — the train appeared to be following them. Strangely, they could not clearly discern the engine in detail, for the haze still surrounded it. Without doubt the train was following them and it had passed over several fog detonators without setting them off. Terror gripped the two men as they ran as fast as they could away from the ghostly train towards Elsham signal box. They burst in on the somewhat startled signalman who was puzzled by the dramatic appearance of the two familiar faces. Ted sank down with relief into a chair.

'Harry,' he gasped. 'There's a strange train on the line coming this way and it has run through all the fogs without setting them off.'

'Get away with you,' replied Harry. 'I've no train on the line. What are you talking about? Just to satisfy you I'll ring Ancholme junction box and see if the signalman knows anything about it. If there had been a train on his section, he would have offered it to me.'

Using his telegraph instrument he communicated with his colleague. No train had been past him and his fogs were out. Harry was convinced that he could account for every train he had accepted.

Their spirits revived by a cup of hot tea, the two men took their leave of the signalman. By now the fog had lifted, but it was so dark that it would have been futile to return to the scene of the mysterious train to discover for themselves any clues as to its reality or otherwise.

Jack and Ted kept their unusual experience to themselves, fearing the ridicule of their friends. It was not until several years later that they were able to unravel the possible cause of the visitation.

One evening in their local pub, the Dog & Rabbit, an old gentleman who had moved out of the district on retirement, returned to visit his daughter who lived in the area. The old man loved to reminisce and would talk for hours about the past. He was a veritable fund of knowledge. Ted and Jack were drawn into conversation with the old man and Ted, remembering the mysterious incident, asked him if he could bring to mind any relevant details. The old man's eyes lit up.

'Yes,' he said. 'I can tell you all about that. It were in the 1920s and it was a passenger train from Cleethorpes to Doncaster and the driver, well, he was a hard, fast driver and he wasn't popular with firemen. This particular day he had a young fireman called Tom Smith, a big strong lad with a fiery temper. The driver, Fred King, used to goad them, always at them, never left them alone so instead of getting the best out of them he seemed to be determined to get the worst instead. This particular day Tom Smith had been out on the drink the previous night and now had a sore head and a filthy mood on him. King was pushing him hard, telling him he was no good and such like, when to King's surprise Smith started to answer back and no one ever did that, so things worsened and it wasn't long before they started fighting, an alarming situation on a small cramped footplate. It is believed that one of them moved the regulator and opened it up with the result that the train was soon out of control. Then reverse curves were coming up and the train ran through the first curve but was going too fast for the next one and the train left the track, killing certainly the driver and fireman and one or two passengers, I believe. A very sad occurrence and such violence. They say that the accident haunts those curves especially in dense fogs, but you'll not worry about that, it's probably an old wives' tale. Anyway, who will have another drink? It's my round.'

31

THE GHOST OF BRADLEY FOLD WEST

The signal box at Bradley Fold West, situated between Bolton and Bury, was a small but important unit miles from anywhere controlling the up and down main lines and both goods loops. It had a cross-over, a set of catch points and four block instruments, two for permissive block working and the other two for absolute block for the main lines. The control exercised from this remote box, therefore, was vital to the smooth operation of this busy line.

Jack Rothera, an ex-Navy man, had wished from his boyhood days to work on the railway. After his demobilisation from the Navy he was accepted by the railway authorities to train as a signalman. His first training began at Bradley Fold West and he soon realised what a wholly essential facet absolute concentration and alertness was about. One slip or lapse and a terrible accident would never be far away. Jack enjoyed his early training and displayed the sort of ability much sought after by the Signal and Telegraph Department. Johnnie Warburton used to work turn-about with him and they enjoyed each other's company. Johnnie also excelled at the job and adapted at the same rate as his friend. Jack well remembers his first shift on his own. He had let a light engine out of the down loop ready to go to Bolton and had refused the bell code for a fast down freight from Bradley Fold station box. He was just telling the driver of the light engine that he would be away in a minute, when from Bradley Fold station box came the 4–5–5 signal (train or vehicles running away on the right line). As the heavy freight train rushed towards his box, the next box down the line at Rose Hill Junction accepted the light engine, telling the driver to accelerate. Jack was able to stop the freight train without accident.

Life for Jack Rothera soon settled into an interesting routine and nothing untoward happened to disturb the smooth operation of his signal box. Johnnie Warburton renewed his acquaintance with Jack when they were designated to work alternate shifts. It was a happy working relationship and each had complete trust in the other's abilities — until Johnnie's happy-go-lucky attitude changed to an unusually quiet and sombre mood. Before long, Johnnie vowed that he would leave the signal box forever.

Jack was puzzled at Johnnie's sudden change in behaviour and although initially he reasoned that his colleague must be troubled with a domestic problem, he could not forget Johnnie's parting words that he intended to leave the box for good. What puzzled Jack was that he himself was very happy at Bradley Fold West and he had settled into the routine and managed the duties without any problems. What could have upset Johnnie? Jack speculated that perhaps there had been some interference by a superior, or that vandals may have seen the lonely outpost as a target for action. Jack had experienced broken windows and other similar nuisances, but nothing else. After much thought and reasoning, however, Jack reached no satisfactory conclusion regarding Johnnie's unhappiness. Nevertheless, he was not prepared to take chances, so he checked and rechecked the security of the box and the store-room below in case vandals from a nearby village might be intending to pay him an unwelcome visit.

A few days later Jack took over the shift at 9pm. At 1.47am he received the bell signal from Rose Hill Junction enquiring if the line was clear for the 2am target train, an express parcels and newspaper train. As all was clear, Jack turned the block over to line clear. Some 2½ minutes later he received the bell code indicating that the train was entering the section. He turned the block over to 'train on line', warned it on to Bradley

Fold Station and pulled his signals off. The train could now be heard coming up the bank. It was going like the wind, as it always did, and in seconds it had passed the box exactly on time, rushing on to Bradley Fold No 3 signal. Having put his signals to danger, and cleared back to Rose Hill Junction that the train was out of section, Jack prepared to book the train's passage in the train register book. As he did so, he heard footsteps passing under the bridge and over the point catwalk and continuing under the box. Remembering Johnnie's warning, Jack concluded that the prowler had come in search of the coal which was stored in bags under the box. Grabbing his torch, he raced down the steps and shone the light into the dark corners, but there was no one to be seen.

The strange occurrence was uppermost in Jack's mind the following night and he determined to catch the intruder if he returned. As on the previous night, the mail train roared past the signal box at the usual time and Jack again heard footsteps in the still night walking under the box. Taking a heavy poker in one hand and a torch in the other, he charged down the steps, feeling certain that the intruder had entered the storeroom. He shone his torch, but as before, no one was there. Feeling frightened, he scurried back up the stairs and sank bewildered into his armchair. Jack was convinced that the uninvited visitor was a light-fingered local looking for free coal. The thought that he might be dealing with a supernatural force did not enter his mind.

Next day Jack pondered the mystery of the unexplained footsteps and laid plans to catch the intruder. On commencing the night-shift, a sinister, inexplicable atmosphere was evident. Jack felt edgy but convinced himself that his nerves were playing tricks on him. He heard strange clicking noises at the windows and footsteps coming up the steps. Flinging open the door, he shone his torch, but nothing stirred. Returning to his chair, he sat and waited. Now he heard a low whistling sound which seemed to come from the rear of the box. With his poker and torch he sought out the noise. He found nothing.

84

An hour later he opened the door and shone his torch. Although the fresh night air was welcome, Jack was again aware of an unusual feeling of dread and foreboding. He had never been afraid or apprehensive before, but now he realised that something was amiss. He closed the door and opened the sliding window in the front of the box looking across the tracks, the clear air showing the gleaming metals of the line. Looking right then left he saw the signals with their warning lights reassuring him of their presence. Suddenly he felt that he was being watched. Turning around quickly he saw a shadow moving across the ceiling light. He pinched himself and warmed his hands on the fire, shuddering against the extremes of the cold night air and the warmth of the signal box. What was the shadow and the feeling of being watched? He looked forward to the end of his shift.

As the mail train thundered past and disappeared into the distance he heard the familiar sound of footsteps. Rushing down the staircase, he turned the corner to the store-room which was fitted with a safety lock requiring four turns of the key. Nobody was there, but the air was heavy with a sense of foreboding. Then an agonising cry rent the still night. Jack hastened to the front of the box shining his torch across the tracks. To his horror, he discerned a recumbent shape at the side of the line. He ran towards it fearing the worst, but to his amazement the figure faded and disappeared as he neared the line side. Baffled and frightened, Jack now understood the significance of Johnnie Warburton's warning. But what was the agonised cry and the figure lying by the line side? Had someone been killed by the mail train? The footsteps, the mysterious whistling noises, the shadows, and the figure that resembled a body lying by the track. Why had he been witness to these events? In a state of nervous confusion, Jack was unable to answer these bewildering questions.

Jack walked slowly back up the stairs numb and shivering. It had turned cold now, but the air remained still. Huddling by the fire he waited impatiently for daylight and his relief. By now Jack was determined to relinquish his night-shift duties.

The thought of undergoing such traumatic experiences was unthinkable.

Years later, Jack was told that some time before his tenure of Bradley Fold West signal box a man from a nearby village was killed on the line. According to reliable sources, but unknown to Jack, at least three other signalmen had experienced the same chain of events, but all had kept their frightening experiences to themselves to avoid the ridicule of their workmates.

32

THE GHOSTLY CARETAKER

Jack Cartwright and his wife June and their two children Alan, 11, and Melissa, 13, had been on a camping holiday in the West Country, but unfortunately everything had gone wrong. The weather had been appalling and as a result the whole family had caught colds. Their misery was complete when the previous night vandals had visited their camp site and caused considerable damage, including slitting the Cartwrights' tent. When the electrics on their normally reliable car had started to fail, Jack and June decided to cut short their holiday and return to their home in South Yorkshire.

Packing up their equipment, they set off home. Their long journey was broken several times by the necessity to make repairs to the car. Darkness began to descend quickly as rainfilled clouds turned the sky to a menacing black void. Before long, the family ran into a ferocious thunderstorm. Driving with difficulty through torrential rain while thunder and lightning crashed overhead, Jack found himself in a narrow West Country lane, realising that he had missed the turning that would have brought him back on to the main road. By now it was dark, they were obviously lost and their headlights had begun to fail. Their only hope was to find a farmhouse where a friendly farmer might be able to offer them shelter for the night.

As they began to despair, their son noticed a railway station sign. Peering through the pouring rain Jack saw a post with an old weather-stained sign hanging from it. As they drove towards their refuge, they found themselves in a large station yard, now overgrown with weeds and bramble bushes and obviously derelict. Like so many abandoned branch-line properties, the dereliction was complete.

The storm had now passed its zenith and although the rain was still pouring down, the Cartwright family felt relieved at finding some form of shelter. Jack drove the car as near as he could towards the station building and switched off the faltering engine. He took a torch with him, left the car and entered the old building. After what seemed an age, Jack appeared out of the gloom and got back into the car.

'I've had a good look round, June,' he said. 'The roof seems sound and I think I can force one of the windows and get in. It's a bit of a mess but at least we can be warm and dry in our sleeping-bags.'

When they reached the building, Jack shone his torch through a broken window illuminating the interior of what evidently had been the booking office. The floor was covered with the rubbish of years, but the place seemed dry and the family's spirits rose. Jack went back to the car for a screwdriver with which he prised open a rotting window.

The family moved in everything they needed to make their stay as comfortable as possible. June lit their camping lamp which cast weird shadows around the room. After a meal, Jack suggested a walk to explore their surroundings. They found a long platform and the remains of a goods shed. The track-bed was weed-ridden and strewn with rubbish. A sense of abandonment overhung the .once proud station. Picking their way through the rubble, the Cartwrights concluded their exploration, although they had no idea of where they were.

As the children walked ahead, Jack and his wife agreed that they could sense a strange atmosphere, something eerie and unpleasant. The children then ran back excitedly to them.

'There's a light in one of the rooms and we've heard voices,' said Melissa.

Their father told them that as they were the only people present in the deserted station, it was not possible to see or hear such things. The children, however, were persistent and led the way round to the side of the building, stopping at what had probably been a small parcels office. Peering through the filthy window, they saw an empty room littered with small rubble, several pieces of broken dust-covered chairs and an old table, but no sign of life. Jack looked at the children.

'But this is the place, Dad,' said Melissa. 'There was a light like an old oil lamp giving a yellow glow, and we heard voices, too.'

Jack believed that they could not be imagining it.

'I know,' he said. 'Let's see if we can get in from the inside as this door is either seized up or securely locked.'

Jack fetched his torch and screw-driver, then climbed through the window, struggling to avoid the broken glass. Marking his way carefully to the door that would give entry to the parcels office, he shone his torch around him. Only dust and rubble showed the years of disuse. Nothing stirred.

After much effort, Jack succeeded in prising open the door with his screw-driver. He shone the torch around the room before entering. No footmarks disturbed the dust, cobwebs hung like festoons and a strange musty smell pervaded the atmosphere. Suddenly he became aware of an eerie feeling, as though he was being watched. Nervously, he stepped into the room and walked around, crunching the broken plaster that had fallen from the crumbling ceiling. There was no one in the room and no oil lamp, but a strange smell pervaded the air. He left the room and was about to close the door behind him when he was hit in the back by the door itself slamming shut. He turned and tried to open the door again, but it was impossible to do so. Feeling frightened by his experience, he was relieved to return to his family in the booking office.

Half an hour later, the Cartwright family were in their sleeping-bags, each of them uneasy and bewildered by the recent strange events. The old building creaked occasionally, but apart from that and the occasional rumble of distant thunder, there was silence.

At about 2am, however, Jack woke with a start. He could

distinctly hear voices which seemed to be coming from the parcels office next door. Quickly putting on some clothes, he decided to investigate.

He tried the door to the parcels office, but it seemed to be locked tightly. The voices were now audible, obviously coming from the room. Jack was determined to solve the mystery. Putting his shoulder to the door, he found to his amazement that it opened easily. Looking inside, he was aware of a misty atmosphere and a figure sitting in a chair at a desk. The voices had stopped now but an illuminating mist seemed to fill the room with a white incandescent glow. The shape of the figure at the desk was vague, but distinctly human. He seemed to be poring over some papers and the room itself appeared to be tidier than when he had visited it earlier. It was as if Jack had stepped back in time to the scene of an earlier age. Suddenly, the figure seemed to be aware of Jack's presence and turned towards him, as if to ask what he wanted. Jack could see the face now, that of an elderly man with a deeply wrinkled face and steel-framed glasses. His face was gentle and benign. As Jack took a step towards the figure the mist suddenly cleared and the figure disappeared. Abruptly, Jack found himself in darkness. He switched on his torch and found himself alone in the office. He was about to shut the door when again an inexplicable force on the other side pushed it firmly shut. Jack again tried the handle, but the door was locked. Totally mystified by his experience, he crept back to the booking hall and tried to sleep.

In the morning, Jack related his experience to his wife who listened sympathetically but reassured him that it must have been a nightmare. As they prepared to leave and resume their homeward journey, Jack decided to take a last look around the parcels office. Gingerly opening the door, which gave way easily, he saw the festoons of cobwebs, litter and crumbling plaster, exactly as before. Satisfied, he gently pulled the door, which closed easily behind him. With a final look back at the station buildings, Jack drove away from the scene of his mysterious experience.

The family's first stop at a garage for a minor repair led Jack into conversation with the proprietor. He told him about their ruined holiday and where they had spent the previous night, although he did not reveal his unusual experience.

The proprietor listened, then said, 'You're a braver man than I am, mister. That station is supposed to be haunted by old Garrity who was that porter there in the old days, and not many people go near it in daylight, never mind after dark.'

Jack laughed. 'Well, he didn't bother me. Perhaps we were lucky.'

33

THE STRANGE VISITOR
OF COVENT GARDEN

The frequent manifestation of a melancholy figure at Covent Garden Underground Station has earned it the unwanted title of the most haunted station on the London Transport system.

The sequence of events began in the early 1960s when Jack Hayden was the station foreman. It was Christmas week (whether this time of the year had any significance or not cannot be explained) and Mr Hayden was in the staff mess room writing up the log book. The time was approximately 12.30am and all was quiet when suddenly the door handle rattled. Mr Hayden looked up from his writing and saw a figure dressed in old-fashioned clothes reminiscent of the style worn at the turn of the century and his expression was one of sadness. Mr Hayden, who at this stage was not thinking of the supernatural, said, 'I think you are lost, sir. The lift to the trains are upstairs.' The stranger made no move. However, when Mr Hayden stood up and made to show the stranger the way, the figure melted into thin air, leaving the foreman completely mystified.

Thinking fatigue had got the better of his tired mind, Jack Hayden did not worry unduly until the following Monday morning when a porter who had been working on the station platform came to the mess room and saw a strange figure looking at Mr Hayden. When the porter entered the room the stranger melted into thin air.

The porter was so terrified that he fainted. On recovery, Mr Hayden described the stranger to the porter who agreed that it was the same figure he had seen. This traumatic experience had such a shattering effect on the porter that he left London Transport for good, swearing never to visit Covent Garden Station again.

Mr Hayden, after further thoughts about the matter, decided to tell the station master, Mr A. Jones, about the occurrence, seeking his advice as to the right measures to adopt in these strange circumstances. Mr Jones suggested that *Physic News* magazine should be approached with a view to investigating the incidents and perhaps providing a satisfactory answer.

Physic News were very interested and one of their researchers visited Jack Hayden and discussed the matter in detail. It was decided that a seance should be held in the mess room and, depending on the result, they would discuss what further measures could be used to identify the ghost. The seance was held and Mr Hayden was later shown some photographs and asked if he could recognise any of the people. After examining the photographs, Mr Hayden recognised William Terris who had been murdered in about 1900 in The Strand which lies just around the corner from Covent Garden Underground Station.

It is thought that William Terris was wearing evening dress, which suggests that he had visited Covent Garden Opera House nearby. However, why his ghost should have been attracted to the station and the area around the mess room has never been explained satisfactorily. William Terris' ghost seemed to have an affinity with Mr Hayden because the foreman saw him nearly every day in some part of the station for some two years. He did not feel afraid of the ghost and tried to speak to him, but the figure was sad and morose as if struck by a remorseless tragedy. *Physic News* told Mr Hayden to talk to the ghost as if to help him, but no response was ever forthcoming.

Eventually, Jack Hayden was promoted to station inspector which made a move away from Covent Garden Station necessary, but he was somewhat frustrated at not being able to re-establish contact with 'Charlie', as he had christened the ghost. However, it appears that many other people were destined to see William Terris, fortunately without any ill effects.

Workmen from the Maintenance Department, which is responsible for the smooth running of the lifts and escalators in the station, have seen William Terris' ghost on numerous occasions as they work mostly at night so that their work causes the least interference with the travelling public. Terris does not seem to mind the electricians who undoubtedly disturb him on his preserve. One gentleman, who has not actually seen the apparition, has on several occasions heard footsteps walking up a stairway in the station. In fact, the uncertain times of Terris' appearances have had such an effect on workmen that the Maintenance Department do not allow their staff to work in the station through the night in case the ghost interferes with their potentially dangerous work. One lady who only saw Terris once would not work in the station again and demanded a move to a 'normal station'.

Jack Hayden obviously has a very close affinity with William Terris' ghost because when he made a purposeful visit to Covent Garden Station recently he saw him 'as large as life', as if waiting to welcome him back.

So it would seem that the ghost of William Terris will haunt Covent Garden Station whenever he pleases, but the object of his frequent appearances will remain a mystery.

34

THE RETURN OF THE
DILIGENT SIGNALMAN

Signal boxes can be very emotive places by virtue of their often remote locations, and inexplicable events have been known to take place in them. Although today these vital units of the railway system are being phased out by the modern fully automated control centres, there still remains the lonely, isolated signal box, often miles from anywhere, that on a dark winter's night can conjure up strange happenings and instil fear even in the heart of the most level-headed signalman.

The signal box at Claxby, 2 miles from Market Rasen in Lincolnshire, is a small box constructed in the GCR type of architecture. It lies ½ mile from the main road to Market Rasen and Lincoln and about 2 miles from the attractive village of Claxby which clings to the ironstone ridge of the Lincolnshire Wolds. The signal box is the setting for an unexplained sequence of events that to this day have puzzled the local authorities. For years, the lonely box had played its part as an essential signal post on the busy main line without anything untoward disturbing its peaceful operation. One night in the early 1960s, however, its tranquillity was upset by strange occurrences.

Aubrey Clark, who for many years had worked his shifts in Claxby box, was on the night turn. Shortly after 5am, the next box along the line, Holton le Moor, contacted Claxby but received no reply. Attempts were made at frequent intervals to contact Mr Clark without success. The signalman at Holton le Moor box felt concerned and stopped the next train entering his section and asked the driver to stop at Claxby and see if everything was in order.

The driver found the box silent and Mr Clark slumped in his armchair, obviously dead. Control was informed of the news and the relief signalman, Ted Hudson who lived in Market Rasen, was summoned to take over the operation of the box. Mr Hudson knew the box intimately and had known Aubrey Clark well. When Ted arrived at the box, the signalman's corpse had been laid out on the signal frame and was covered with a sheet, from where he was removed by ambulance to the local hospital. The signals were at caution and the train crew were talking on the level-crossing. Ted resumed the operation of the cabin and tried to shake off the depressing atmosphere that now pervaded the small room.

Mr J. Daubney, who was a relief signalman at Wrawby and Barnetby, relieved Ted at about 5.30pm. As Daubney felt that the box reeked of death, Ted decided to burn Aubrey's old armchair and replace it with another to remove the visible signs of the tragedy. Mr Daubney was in charge of the box for the rest of that week but felt uneasy. He rang Holton le Moor frequently to talk to someone, fearing that the lonely hours would revive the still recent memories of the death of Aubrey Clark.

The following week, Ted Hudson undertook the 6pm to 6am shift. The first two nights passed uneventfully, but on the third night, Ted heard the sound of heavy breathing which seemed to come from the armchair. When he rose and looked around, the breathing stopped. He walked to the door and looked out, but no one was there and all was still. But when he returned to the chair and sat down, the breathing started again. Ted convinced himself that the sounds came from the birds nesting in the eaves or the rafters and banged the walls with a brush. The wooden walls shook and the alien noise echoed around the small building, and for a while the noise stopped. After a while, however, the heavy stertorous breathing began again. The sound was louder now and seemed to fill the box. Impatiently, Ted went outside with a brush and prodded the eaves to drive out any birds that might be disturbing his peace. However, not a single bird flew out. On returning to the box and resuming his duties, he was more puzzled than frightened for he did not believe in ghosts.

The following night the same sound disturbed his normally peaceful night-shift and as he could find no logical explanation he decided to accept whatever it was, but resolved to keep the mystery to himself to avoid the ridicule of his workmates.

On his last night-shift of the week, Ted had been told that the platelaying gang would be undertaking essential track repairs near the box starting at midnight. Unknown to Ted, however, this work had been postponed.

It was a moonlight night and from 11pm Ted was waiting for the platelayers' arrival as their company would liven his long shift. Almost at midnight, he was disturbed by a terrific kick on the door. Thinking that it was the platelayers playing a joke on him, he said 'Come in', but no one entered. He had hardly sat down again when there was another strong kick at the door. 'Come in,' he repeated, but again no one entered. Somewhat perturbed, Ted flung the door open still believing that the platelayers were playing tricks on him. He looked outside and there at the bottom of the steps was Aubrey Clark dressed in his motor-cycle gear, his helmet glinting in the moonlight. (Aubrey, in fact, travelled to work on a motor scooter. On reaching the box, he would take off his helmet and put it over one arm, while his tuck-box was held under the other. He would then climb the steps and on reaching the top would kick the door and whoever was on duty would open the door for him.) Ted stood and stared at the apparition in amazement, unable to believe the sight of his old friend before his eyes. Then the vision faded, leaving Ted feeling totally bemused.

A few weeks later, Ted relieved Bob Webster at about 5.45am. Bob, normally a level-headed signalman, looked ill at ease and asked Ted if he had heard any strange noises in the box. The two men exchanged experiences and found that they had heard the same noises of heavy breathing and the kick on the door. Both agreed that there would seem to be no rational explanation, but everything pointed to the fact that Aubrey Clark was revisiting his old signal box. Other signalmen had similar stories to tell and some refused to work the box, so frightened were they of the strange events. One snowy morning footprints and tyre marks were imprinted in the snow even though Ted had received no visitor at the box.

By day, Claxby signal box is warm and friendly and it is difficult to believe that any mysterious events could take place there. But Ted Hudson and other signalmen like him know that in the early hours of a winter's morning a visitation from Aubrey Clark's ghost is a real and frightening possibility.

35

THE HEADLESS LOVER

The gruesome story of the headless lover began early in the 1900s when Brooke End signal box controlled the up and down main lines, an up goods loop and sidings used by the pick-up trains of that period.

Not far from the railway line lived a closely knit family, Mr and Mrs Gorman and their only daughter, Marion. Gorman worked on the Railway as a platelayer and as such, occupied a small cottage maybe 200yd away from the main line. It was small, but adequate for the Gormans' needs and comforts, built in the Midland Railway's style of architecture having a pantile roof and very solidly constructed of red brick. A large meadow lay in front of it and from the sash windows views of the rural countryside could be enjoyed. Marion loved her home and its cosy atmosphere gave the shy girl great assurance. She was a beautiful girl of average height, fine boned and blue eyed. Her long flaxon hair gave her an almost nordic appearance, her clear unspoilt complexion reflecting her life in the clean country air.

Marion was born in this cottage and had long become used to the passage of trains and shunting movements in the adjacent sidings. She had few friends in the locality, preferring to go for long walks in the nearby countryside with the family dog, until, that is, Ronald Travis took up his duties in the signal box. He was in his late twenties, of average height, had fair hair and blue eyes, was of stocky build and self sufficient. He had proved an enthusiastic pupil when learning the complicated tedious job of a signalman. He did not mind the night-shifts or the tedium of the long lonely hours. His practical disposition and dependability were appreciated by his colleagues who welcomed his cheerfulness. Ronald was a country lad, interested in the country ways and traditions.

Marion met him one night when he called to see her father on a matter appertaining to the permanent way adjacent to the signal box. For Marion and Ronald it was love at first sight. They spent all their spare time together and the courtship developed rapidly. Marion adored him and they enjoyed many happy, carefree walks together. Mr and Mrs Gorman at first were relieved that their only child had found such a solid, trustworthy young man and in fact encouraged the relationship, until Marion began to disappear for hours and then return home without saying where she had been. Travis would not give any explanation when asked about her whereabouts and seemed to resent her parents' questions.

One night Mr Gorman remembered that he had to visit the box to give Travis a message about the next week's duty roster. Sighing at the thought of having to leave the warmth and comfort of the fire, he rose and lifted his coat from the hook on the kitchen door, bracing himself against the cold stormy air, and strode off into the darkness. Approaching the signal box he mounted the steps, the hand-rail creaking as he used it for support. All was quiet. The silence was explained, however, as he entered the box and found Marion and Ronald in a deep embrace, their feelings for each other so apparent. It was now obvious where Marion was spending so much of her time. Mr Gorman felt angry. The girl was betraying the trust that her parents had instilled into her all her young life. He realised that Marion's reticence was to protect the secret of her love affair with Ronald Travis. Mr Gorman lost his temper and accused Travis of luring away his daughter. In spite of the couple's protestations, he forbade Marion to meet Travis again and firmly escorted his tearful daughter home.

From then on, Marion became morose and irritable. Life

became difficult in the erstwhile happy home and the unfortunate girl was only allowed to go for walks in the company of her parents. One night, after a violent row, Marion ran up to her room and locked the door. Her parents, visibly upset, decided to allow her to calm down and not to disturb her. Marion, in her distressed, emotional state, was sobbing in bed. She could not sleep and, remembering that Ronald Travis would be on duty, decided to wait until her parents had gone to bed, then slip outside and go to the signal box to see her lover. It was a dark night and she lay quietly until she was satisfied that her parents were asleep. Then, dressing in her long white dress, she stole quietly downstairs and made her way down the path to the gate and across the meadow to the railway line. The all-enveloping darkness made her progress difficult but in her emotional state she staggered on. Reaching the railway fence she climbed over and started across the tracks. In the distance she could hear a train coming and could see the yellow lights of the oil lamps in the signal box. The oncoming train drew nearer. She was gasping, but she knew she could beat it if she ran. She had not much further to go and soon she would be safe in her lover's arms.

Safely over the down line, she started to cross the up line, but stumbled and fell. With the train rapidly bearing down on her she did not stand a chance. The vigilant driver, seeing her white-clad body almost in front of his engine, applied his brakes and slammed shut the regulator. He and his fireman felt the terrifying impact. The engine passed over her, the wheels severing her head from her body. By this time Travis was on the horrible scene of the accident, the bloodstained white dress revealing a gruesome sight. Travis raced to the Gormans' cottage and with great difficulty told the distressed couple what had happened.

The ensuing enquiries and inquest returned a verdict of accidental death and the sad interlude closed, apparently the end of a tragic love affair.

Travis was transferred to another area and the life of the signal box returned to normal. Then, in the late 1940s a series of incidents happened that have no logical explanation and caused distress and horror.

At dawn one spring morning a heavily loaded freight train, headed by a pre-war 2–8–0 locomotive, was running out of steam owing to a badly clinkered fire-bed as it approached Brook End signal box. The signalman, knowing that this train had been in his section for some time and was overdue, set his points and signal from the up main to the up goods loop to allow the up passenger train, following the goods, to run past without any unnecessary delay. As the freight train came slowly to a halt at the loop stop signal near the box, the fireman told the signalman of their problem who in turn reported the incident to the train control. The engine driver also gave control some idea of how long it would take to clean the fire and raise sufficient steam for him to take his train forward.

Meanwhile, the train guard, George Marsh, decided to make himself a mug of tea. Standing on the brake-van verandah, he looked down the line towards the signal box. Suddenly he saw a white figure slowly crossing the main line towards Brooke End signal box. She was obviously taking a risk as the up passenger train was almost due and up main signals had been switched to off. In fact, the approaching train was already audible. He jumped down quickly from his brake-van and ran down the line shouting a warning. The figure, that of a young girl dressed in a white dress, appeared to stumble and fall and then, as he drew nearer, she rose to her feet and staggered towards the signal box steps. He stopped dead in his tracks, rooted to the spot with horror. The white-clad figure had no head and there were blood-stains on the front of her dress. The horrific headless figure disappeared as it reached the foot of the steps. On hearing George Marsh shout, then scream, those in the box looked out and saw momentarily the terrifying apparition seconds before it disappeared. The driver was the first to recover his scattered wits and went down the steps to comfort Marsh who was leaning against the tender side, shaking uncontrollably, his face ashen. He assisted Marsh up the steps to the box and, seating him in the signalman's battered but comfortable old armchair, reported the incident to the train control, requesting medical assistance for the unfortunate guard who was obviously unable to continue his duties.

So ended one of the most traumatic experiences ever seen on the railway system in the British Isles. Others who have had the misfortune to witness the headless apparition wish to remain anonymous. Their memories are so vivid and horrific that they wish to forget them.

With the modernisation of the railway system, Brooke End signal box was abandoned, its structure left to stand forlorn. The windows had long ago been broken and the inside of the box had been completely vandalised. Dark, scorched areas suggested that an unsuccessful attempt had been made to set fire to it. The box seemed resigned to its fate of demolition. When that day came, perhaps the tragic story of a love-sick young girl trying to find solace in the arms of her lover would be laid to rest forever.

36

THE UNSEEN PRESENCE OF
GRIMSBY FISH DOCKS

This totally unexplained mystery took place in the 1950s in a siding that ran parallel to Fish Dock Road, a main arterial road leading on and off Grimsby Fish Docks. The railway line ran between various buildings and a high wooden fence that was used for part of its length for advertisement hoardings. Railwaymen who worked in the area had been so overcome by a feeling of evil that pervaded a particular location that they refused to work the night-shift that involved going near the place in question.

It was the custom of the train crews to make up the fish trains from empty stock located in the New Clee sidings, between Grimsby and Cleethorpes. From there the vans would be collected by the ex-Great Central Railway Fish Dock tankers (a little outside cylinder 0–6–0 side tank locomotive of a short-wheel base design for working the tight curves on the docks) and pushed up the fish jetty for loading with fish for despatch to such places as Leicester and Banbury as part of the express fish train service offered by the railway.

One Monday night around midnight, some thirty-five vans had been brought up from New Clee sidings, pushed down Melhuish's Jetty, loaded up, and were brought back to the middle road alongside Fish Dock Road. One of the shunters who rode on the engine then alighted, went down the train to connect up the vacuum pipes known to the railwaymen as vacuum bags.

The night was dark and still and the middle road had an eerie, forbidding atmosphere. The street light threw strange shadows among the hoardings. The shunters shuddered as they went about their work. That particular night seemed strangely different, and inexplicably the dark shadows seemed even more menacing than usual.

When the 'bags' had been connected and the brake was continuous through the train the engine driver would 'blow up' the vacuum to get the required 21in, thus creating the correct pressure on the vacuum gauge. On this occasion he could only get 5in so he told one of the shunters, George Dyson, what had happened and asked him to go back along the fish vans and find out if a bag was off. Armed with a lamp, Dyson set off to check the connection.

'Have you found anything?' asked the driver.

Mr Dyson shook his head.

'Everything's all right. Try your pressure now,' he said.

But the dial still only showed 5in.

'There's still something wrong,' said the driver.

Jack St Pierre, another shunter on the same gang, was asked to go and check the bags. He slowly made his way along the train of fish vans. In spite of his powerful torch, the darkness seemed to close in on him and he felt a weird, evil presence as if something would spring out from between the silent waggons and overpower him. He shone his torch on the connections. The light seemed to dim and was not reassuring. About three-quarters of the way down the train Jack began to feel very frightened for the overpowering sense of impending evil became even stronger. Yet he still could not find the offending bag. He felt his nerve breaking and terror began to overtake his mind. A horrible damp stifling smell then filled his lungs. Jack could go no further and he turned and ran terrified back to the engine. Fighting for breath he called up to the driver, 'I can't find anything amiss,' and then walked towards his workmates who were standing talking.

Once more the driver tried the vacuum and again could only

get 5in. By this time, he was obviously annoyed. 'Come here, you lot,' he said. 'Now, what's going on? There must be a bag off somewhere. How is it you can't find it?'

The men stared silently at each other, then one plucked up courage and said, 'There's something not quite right down there,' pointing to the line of fish vans.

The driver, now glowing with impatience, agreed volubly, 'You're absolutely right,' he snarled. 'I can't get any vacuum pressure. What's the matter with you? Have you seen a ghost or something?'

Mr Dyson replied, 'No, we haven't seen a ghost. But I can't explain it, it's as if the devil himself is down there, and there's this horrible smell that chokes you and at the same time you get the feeling that something evil is lying in wait for you. And another thing, the torch goes dim as if it's losing its power. It's so frightening, I'm scared and I'm not going back there — I just don't know what's going on.'

His mates nodded and one said, 'I agree with George, I've never known such a feeling of evil and I am not risking my neck for anyone.' He switched on his torch and the powerful beam clove the darkness like a white spear. 'See that,' he said. 'Nothing's wrong with the torch now, but down there it nearly went out.'

The driver, now totally exasperated, climbed down from the engine. 'Now look, I'll come with you. Pass me the torch, Mick. Now we'll see what's going on.'

The men set off in fear and trepidation, singing and whistling to bolster their courage. The driver led the way, turning around periodically to check that the others were with him. Nearing the end of the line of vans the driver was aware to his surprise of a feeling of dread pervading the atmosphere. He turned to find the shunters huddled together. 'Come on, let's look for this bag,' he said. Unenthusiastically, the men shone their torches around the couplings and flexible connections, but each and everyone of them was aware of the overpowering feeling of evil. Eventually the offending bag was found and re-connected by trembling hands. Their duty done, the whole gang ran as fast as possible back to the engine and gathered in the cab. After they had regained their breath and composure, they all swore that they would never again frequent that evil place. Investigation failed to produce any reason why such an evil atmosphere should pervade that area. Now the track has gone and a road covers the scene.

Many years later, but before the tracks were removed, a tragic event happened on the line. A well-known member of a prominent fishing company whose life had been plagued by tragedy and illness decided to commit suicide. On the particular afternoon he decided to end his life he had been watching the marshalling of the fish vans from his office window. He waited for the right moment, walked calmly across the road, knelt down, put his neck across the railway line and waited for a loaded van to sever his head. The forces of evil must have been working smoothly that day because it so happened that the spot he chose was the position within yards of the epicentre of terror that had frightened the railwaymen so many years earlier. One is left to wonder if the malevolent unseen spirit was waiting to claim its victim, having been unable to satisfy its evil appetite. However, nothing untoward has happened at that spot since and the lines have been lifted, affording no clue as to the evil influence that lurked under the hoardings of the Fish Dock Road.

37

'ARNOLD' AND THE
GREEN MORRIS MINOR

In the first premonition, Mr Reynolds saw himself standing on the footplate of No 43106 leaving Bridgnorth, smoke-box first, with some covered wagons heading for Bewdley. As the cab began to cross the bridge, the first full-span cross-beam collapsed as a green Morris Minor car was passing underneath. The cab was filled with steam and flame as the engine fell through the bridge. At this point the premonition ended.

Mr Reynolds' second premonition again took place on the footplate of No 43106 leaving Bridgnorth. He saw himself look back along the train and then remember the first premonition. He realised the impending danger and looked up the road where he saw a Morris Minor coming down the hill. He told the driver to stop as the bridge was going to collapse. When he refused, Mr Reynolds climbed off the engine and watched it fall through the bridge on to the car, steam and smoke erupting from the cab as it did so. The first wagon fell on to the wreckage and so the premonition ended.

The third and final premonition was situated on the corner of the castle walk. Mr Reynolds saw an engine leaving Bridgnorth and a green Morris Minor coming down the hill towards the bridge. As the cab of the engine moved on to the bridge the engine fell through, the cab falling first, on to the car that was passing underneath.

Mr Reynolds related these premonitions solely to his wife

Ruth. A few weeks later Mr Walker told Ruth of a premonition that he had had the previous night — it was identical to Mr Reynolds'. The latter decided that it was time to visit the bridge and examine the suspect area.

He discovered loose rivets and serious fretting which had occurred between the main beam and the first three cross-beams on the right-hand side only. The bridge had been cleaned and repainted two years earlier and was found to be sound. At the time, Mr Reynolds himself had looked out of curiosity and everything seemed to be in order. On discovering the fretting, he informed the chief civil engineer who imposed a strict speed limit on the bridge.

A new bridge was fitted some three months later during the winter. About six months after Mr Reynolds' first premonition, he experienced unexplained noises, mainly thumping and banging. One night he and his wife witnessed a vague aura of human form on the fire-box top of No 43106. It lasted about a minute before fading and they both sensed a feeling of impending danger. After the bridge was repaired, 'Arnold', as they named the apparition, disappeared. Mr Reynolds believes that he was a ghost of the future, possibly of someone who was not supposed to die should the bridge collapse — in other words, the driver of No 43106, the driver of the green Morris Minor or Mr Reynolds himself.

On another occasion, Mr Reynolds had just gone to bed when he had the feeling that there was a fire on the site. He dressed himself, borrowed a torch and went outside. He walked along Platform 2 and noticed smoke coming from the signal box. By the time he reached the box, the first flames had started. Although the fire was put out in twenty minutes, about £3,000 worth of damage was done, mainly to the electrical system and interlocking mechanism.

Whether Arnold could be blamed for the fire, Mr Reynolds could not be sure, but his comings and goings certainly seemed to leave a trail of mystery and unease. For him, Bridgnorth would always be associated with the antics of a ghost that obviously liked railway engines and would appear from time to time to warn of impending accidents.

38

THE MYSTERIOUS PASSENGER

One morning, a gentleman left Euston Station, London, with some important papers which he intended to read on his journey. The guard found him an empty compartment and locked the door. As the train was departing, an elderly man hurriedly boarded and entered the compartment where the solitary occupant was studying his documents. The two men eventually fell into conversation, the late-comer explaining that he was a director of the railway company and that he was interested in a new branch line that was to be opened. He was also carrying £70,000 which he was depositing in a bank for payment for the work that had just been completed. The late-comer said to his travelling companion, 'By the way, I know the house that you are visiting. The lady of it is my niece. Tell her that I hope the next time I come to stay she won't have such a huge fire in the Blue Room.'

As the train was approaching the director's station, he rose to his feet and drew from his pocket a visiting card bearing the name Dwerringhouse which he gave to his fellow traveller. After he had left the train, the remaining passenger noticed a cigar-case lying on the floor. He picked it up and ran out on to the platform hoping to return it to its owner. He managed to catch a brief glimpse of him talking to a man at the end of the platform. The man's hair was sandy in colour and his face was distinctly visible. However, unaccountably the two men disappeared and a porter was unable to help as he had not seen either of the two people. The gentleman returned to his compartment and resumed his journey, puzzled by his strange experience.

Having reached his destination, he remembered the message that he had been asked to give to his hostess: 'I travelled down with an uncle of yours and he told me to give you the following message,' he said. Both the lady and her husband were obviously distressed at the message regarding the huge fire in the Blue Room. When the ladies retired, the husband explained that the message had been very embarrassing to his wife since her uncle had disappeared with £70,000 and the police were looking for him. It so happened that directors of the railway company who were house guests overheard this conversation and subsequently asked him if he would appear before the board and tell the story of his journey and travelling companion.

In due course the meeting took place. As he was relating his story, he suddenly realised that sitting before him among the directors was the sandy-haired man he had seen talking to Mr Dwerringhouse. The latter, a cashier with the company, immediately protested his innocence and said that he had been away on holiday at the time. However, the directors insisted that the cashier's records should be examined and it soon became clear that there were discrepancies in the accounts. The cashier eventually broke down and confessed that he had accidentally killed Mr Dwerringhouse knowing that he would be carrying £70,000. He intended to use the cash to repay the money he had stolen from the company. He had waylayed Mr Dwerringhouse and hit him on the head to stun him, but in falling to the ground, the older man had hit his head on a large stone and sustained a fatal blow.

The curious episode of the cigar-case was also explained. Owing to some essential repairs, the carriage in which Mr Dwerringhouse had travelled had been out of use from the day of his journey to his subsequent ghostly appearance. The guard at Euston was positive that on that particular day he had locked the door of the compartment and that there was only one gentleman inside when the train left the station.

39

THE LOUTH–BARDNEY
PHANTOM GOODS TRAIN

In order to explain fully the story of the Louth–Bardney goods train it is necessary to describe the line's history and situation. Louth in Lincolnshire, 16 miles south of Grimsby, is a pleasant little country market town. With the formation of the East Lincolnshire Railway Company in 1848, Louth became an important junction, for in 1874, together with other branch lines, it became like the hub of a wheel, with its main line from Grimsby to Boston, Spalding and Peterborough running north and south, the branch going south-east to Sutton on Sea, Mablethorpe and Skegness, and the Louth–Bardney branch going west through the Lincolnshire Wolds towards Bardney and Lincoln. The latter is the branch line on which the mysterious ghost train was heard. It was planned to be an important branch, conveying iron ore from the strata at Apley and Donington, but this traffic never materialised owing to the vast amount of iron ore deposits found at Santon, near Scunthorpe. However, the branch in its sylvan setting and meandering through the scenic beauty of the Wolds was often called the 'Bluebell Line'. It became a boon to the farming community, being used extensively to convey agricultural products and large amounts of sugar beet to the large sugar-beet processing factory at Bardney.

When it first opened, the service operated 8 passenger trains a day, 4 up and down and 2 daily goods, 6 days a week. Patrick

Stirling was the locomotive engineer of the GNR. As was common with branch lines, engines of an older and secondary nature would be used; thus, Sturrocks 0–6–0 tender engines were known to operate on the goods and sometimes the passenger trains. Later, of course, engines of the Stirling and Ivatt vintage found their way down the single line branch. Passenger traffic was never profitable, but it was a link between the two towns to be used by the sparse population as and when required. In World War I the traffic increased by way of the requirements of the armed forces, as it did during World War II. A great deal of traffic was involved in moving ammunition and bombs for the many airfields in the vicinity. After World War II, the motor car had a significant impact on the travelling public, and lorries and buses took a considerable amount of business from the railway, so it was inevitable that the railway management, casting a critical eye over branch line expenditure, however scenic, considered most of these rural lines as financially unviable. In 1951, therefore, the last passenger train ran on the Louth–Bardney line. Freight services ran until 1956 when all services ceased and the track was lifted as far as Bardney, although the Bardney–Lincoln portion remained.

Although this seemed to be the end of the Louth–Bardney line, it refused to die. It seemed as if some supernatural force was intent on operating the branch. At Hallington (the first station from Louth) people heard sounds of a distant train approaching the village. It was rumoured that the 'train' actually came into Hallington Station and blew off steam (even though the track had been lifted for some years).

Having heard the stories, the author decided to investigate them for himself together with a friend. One night in August 1969, therefore, the two men drove to Hallington to reconnoitre the line. They found that the track-bed was still in good condition and that the well-preserved station house was inhabited by a local shepherd. On the subject of the ghost train, the shepherd was not prepared to make any comment. The two friends took stock of everything in the immediate vicinity. On their left was a field of sheep; to their right was a grass field which appeared to be uninhabited.

It was a perfect summer's night, warm and still. At 11.45pm the two men listened and waited in silence. Then they heard the unexpected faint sound of a train, seemingly working hard, possibly on a short cut-off. The sound became louder until the occasional snatch of wagon couplings and the unmistakable clank of side rods could be heard. So fascinated, intrigued and frightened were the two men by this unusual experience, that they listened without uttering a word. The sound seemed to come in waves, getting louder and louder, then fading away. For what seemed an age, they felt gripped with terror and unable to move. They were mesmorised by the ethereal sound. Then, as if to break the spell, the sheep dogs began to bark frenziedly and the nearby sheep stampeded as if they sensed impending danger.

The sheep eventually settled down, and the dogs' barking receded into whimpering. The men strained their ears for continuing sounds of the ghostly train. It had receded on a faint wave of sound, but it was possible to imagine it working hard against the up-grade of the Withcall tunnel cutting. Gradually, even the faintest sound died away. The sheep became placid once again and the dogs were quiet, probably asleep.

The two friends discussed their experience on the way home. They checked their notes. They had not been dreaming. They had heard a train without doubt. What had startled the dogs whose frenzied barking had disturbed the sheep? The visitation of the phantom train had made the dogs aware of an unusual happening. Why had the train run again? Was it the call of a soul in torment? Why had the two men been favoured with a sound of the supernatural? Of the reason for this incredible experience, there can be little doubt that it was the supernatural echoes of the train which once ran along that peaceful little branch line.

Others who visited the line subsequently to share the experience were not favoured to witness the sound of the ghostly train. A local farmer had installed a grain-drier in the immediate locality which may have prevented any such mani-festation from being heard.

Reliable reports have been received since 1969 that the ghostly train runs along the old Louth–Bardney line, all accounts bearing witness to this remarkable phenomenon.

40

THE GHOSTS OF ROTHLEY STATION

Stuart Bailey, station master of Rothley on the Great Central Railway, has heard many stories of ghosts which have appeared at his station, although he himself has no first-hand experience of the supernatural.

One tale was told to him as recently as August 1983. The story began when a young man attended a party in Mournacre Hill, a suburb of Leicester. It was very late when he left the party, and as he was unable to obtain transport to his home in Mountsorrel, he decided to walk along the old track-bed from Belgrave to Rothley Station, this being the most direct route home. In view of what occurred later, one may believe that the young man was intoxicated. However, undoubtedly the night air would have had a sobering effect, especially as the walk was some 2¾ miles long. Being the dead of night, the man was uncertain of how to leave the railway and at Rothley he walked up on to the platform. There by the light of an adjoining street lamp he clearly saw the figure of a station master or porter wearing a flat-topped regulation hat apparently waiting for a train. This was at about 2am on a Sunday morning and the sight of the apparition frightened him. The young man ran across the goods yard and eventually found the gate on to the road. On relating the story to Mr Bailey, the man asked whether a train service was running at that time of night. The answer was negative.

Another well known and frequently reported story is that of the man and his dog at Swithland. If one looks at a map of the line, bridge No 352 carried the country road from Rothley plain to Swithland village, beneath the line at Swithland sidings. The next bridge to the south, No 354, is that at Rothley Station ½ mile away. The missing bridge is not a mystery in itself and one can see traces of the formation of the structure at the far end of Swithland cutting about ¾ mile north of the station. It was a farm occupation bridge under the railway connecting Swithland Lane to the east of the line with fields to the west. The bridge was filled in some twenty or thirty years ago when houses spread along this part of Swithland Lane.

Before World War II, a local man had some pens in the field on the western side of the line in which he reared pigs and poultry. In midwinter the track beneath this bridge became a muddy morass, so at night, when he could not be seen by the signalman in Swithland box, he and his dog, who were inseparable, used to cross over the railway lines. Inevitably, one night in the early years of the war, both he and his dog were killed by a passing train. From then on until the closure years, both man and dog were seen on many occasions from Swithland signal box and the platform at Rothley Station.

Strange figures have also appeared at the arcaded station entrance stairs at Rothley Station, so the area seems to be favoured by visitations of ghostly phenomena.

41

EVENTS IN LINCOLNSHIRE
SIGNALBOXES

The Noise in the Night

Elsham signalbox is situated in a very remote part of the Lincolnshire countryside and thus evokes more strange happenings that baffled John Daubney when he had to take over the box as a relief signalman. One nightshift in particular had mysterious overtones and still has not been explained.

Mr Daubney had been busy with a continuous stream of traffic. When he was able to sit down for a brief breather, he received a telephone call from control saying that some twenty young bullocks had got loose on the railway line heading in his direction and would he keep a look out, with the thought that trains and cattle do not mix. As it was very nearly dark, he did not relish the thought of trying to catch panic stricken young bullocks on a railway line. He did not see any sign of the runaway animals but later on that night the local policeman called on him and he took over the task of keeping a look out.

When the constable called, he left his bicycle leaning against the signalbox wall and it screeched a little way along the wall before coming to a rest; the sound was to remain in Mr Daubney's memory for reasons that will be revealed. The constable stayed with John Daubney for the rest of his shift and the signalman appreciated his company, but with no sign of the errant beasts and although both men peered regularly into the darkness and even went down to the lineside and checked, nothing was to be seen. Hopefully the cattle had been rounded up and were now safe.

The next night John Daubney resumed the nightshift. No cattle to worry about tonight he thought and settled down to the job in hand. Everything was normal and the shift going smoothly until about 3 a.m. when the human body is at its lowest ebb (according to the medical profession) and we don't feel at our best. John heard a noise just like Constable Hobbs' bicycle screeching down the side of the box until it met an obstacle on the wall and stopped or that is what it sounded like in the stillness of the night. 'Good', thought the signalman, 'the policeman has called and it will be nice to have someone to say Hello to.' He went to the door, opened it and looked down the steps expecting to see the burly figure of the constable emerge and climb the steps to meet him, but to John's surprise there was nobody at all. He went round the corner of the building shining his lamp but nothing was to be seen.

'Strange', he thought, and started to puzzle out what the noise could have been caused by. He resolved that the occurrence could be sorted out in daylight and that there was no point in groping about in the dark. Once back upstairs in the box, he could not leave the mystery alone and his mind conjured up all sorts of solutions but analysing them brought no relief. When he was relieved by the early turn man to take over the daylight duties, he mentioned the strange incident and asked him if he had any experiences to relate. The other could think of nothing to tell to either corroborate or add to the mystery. John later came back to the box and searched around the land round the cabin to look for explanations but no solution presented itself and the mystery remains to this day and defies rational belief.

John Daubney is no fool and has sought the solution because he, like many others, looks for reasons for unexpected noises occurring at 3 a.m. in the morning.

Black Shuck's Revenge

Places of human burial, be they cemeteries or church

graveyards or Ancient Briton, Roman or Saxon burial barrows or mounds, are usually regarded as worthy of respect and reverence. To disturb the resting place of any person is regarded as defiling the dead and fortunately, not too many cases are recorded, but one type of archaeological exploration can quite accidentally set off a very volatile and dangerous sequence of events that, on this occasion, cost a man his life and left a whole community in a traumatic turmoil.

Ted Smith owned a smallholding in a remote village in South Lincolnshire. He was able to live quite comfortably from the fruits of his labours but he had always wanted just a little more land. Next to his acreage was a small field of one and a half acres with a little mound in it. Ted felt this field would be very useful and would enable him to extend his holding just sufficient to give him in his words, 'that bit extra'. The trouble was that the land belonged to a family who lived in London and owned parcels of land all over the country and had so far resisted all attempts to relinquish this innocuous piece of British soil.

Ted had given up all hope of enlarging his holding and was concentrating his efforts on farming his existing soil, making a reasonable living from his multiplicity of vegetable crops, when a letter arrived one day explaining to him that if he still wanted to buy the adjoining land, the owners were interested in discussing the matter. Ted acted quickly and in time a deal was concluded and he became the owner of one and a half acres of grassland.

After careful consideration Ted decided to deep plough the land and prepare it for cultivation. One morning, Ted drove a tractor and plough into the field and commenced the job. The land was hard and compacted but the plough shares carved through the earth cleanly and Ted knew his labours wouldn't be wasted. Suddenly, Ted was aware that he was ploughing up something other than earth. He stopped, switched the ignition off and climbed down. Turning round he saw a litter of bones strewn among the furrows. 'Good Lord', he thought, 'I've hit a graveyard!' On examination of the bones he decided that they were very old and the smell that exuded was particularly obnoxious.

Ted decided to stop the operation and return home to discuss the find with his wife, Maureen, whose counsel was always common sense. Maureen was adamant. 'Leave them alone until someone who understands them has examined the site. Besides they may be some value or of interest to a museum, you never know.' Ted agreed but he decided to go and discuss the matter with his pal, Jim, who was the local signalman.

Jim was very interested and liked a mystery. He was also very curious and begged Ted to allow him to have a look round. Their discussion was interrupted by the visit of Ted's Uncle Albert, who, at the age of 81, had wisdom to offer about most things. He was put into the picture and was asked his opinion. 'You have disturbed a burial site all right but what is important is that you don't disturb it further,' he advised. Jim was still curious. 'What about any valuables that may be buried with the remains? Could we get the archaeologists here for a dig?' Uncle Albert shrugged his shoulders. 'It's up to Ted. It's his land but if I were you both, I wouldn't disturb the dead, very dangerous!' Ted laughed. 'Good Lord, what could the bones to do us? I'm not frightened, are you Jim?' Jim smiled. 'It could be very interesting, I like a mystery.' Uncle Albert sighed. 'Well, I've warned you, don't meddle in things you don't understand.'

That night, Ted and Jim met in the local pub to discuss the situation. Jim said, 'How about having another look at the site? We may uncover some valuables. It could be a Roman or Saxon burial ground and they were buried with their treasures. Perhaps we might uncover something of interest!' Ted finished his drink. 'OK, we'll have another look but don't tell anyone else or we'll have the whole village digging it up.'

The following morning, Jim was free and the two men stood looking at the bones. 'They smell a bit, Ted,' said Jim. Ted felt an inexplicable shudder. 'Something unpleasant about the whole affair don't you think?' Jim was excited. 'Come on,' he urged, 'let's see what else we can find.' The two men started to dig down among the scattered bones to find other signs of interest. The work was hard and the sweat ran off their brows. They took great care and were concentrating on a small area, trying hard not to tread on the bones. After a lot of hard work, they found they were uncovering a more or less intact skeleton. As they uncovered it, they found they were looking at not a human, but an animal. Not a cow or horse but the size of a sheep or goat. With continued care they exposed an intact skeleton. They rested and looked and sweated. 'What is it?' gasped Ted. Jim thought and gazed. 'Well, it looks like a large dog, look at its head.' The head was large and flattened, resembling a labrador or retriever. 'Tell you what,' said Jim, 'I'll take the skull and show it to Dave, the vet. He'll know what it could be.' Ted agreed. 'Come on, let's go and have a cup of tea. Maureen was getting on to the museum about bringing an expert to have a look at the place.'

Maureen had some news. 'I've been in touch with the museum and someone is coming over next week and in the meantime they said don't touch anything.' Ted explained that they had uncovered more bones including the animal. He laughed, 'Jim's got the skull, he's going to show it to Dave, the vet.' Maureen frowned, 'Do you think that's wise?' Jim giggled. 'Course it's all right. It won't bite me. Anyway, I must be off. Thanks for the tea.' Early the next morning, Jim was on duty in the signalbox. He had the skull in a plastic bag ready to consult Dave Smith, the local vet, when his shift ended. During a lull in the rail traffic, he opened the bag and had a good look at the object. It was hideous and awesome; it must have been a big animal. The jaws were large and powerful. Jim shuddered and put it back in the bag. Somehow he kept thinking about the whole affair and he wasn't sure anymore about the skull; should he have moved it?

When his shift ended, Jim made his way to Dave's surgery. Dave examined the skull and sucked his teeth. 'Must have been something big. I'd say it was a dog but it's very, very old and that's as much as I can tell. I should put it back and cover it up.

No point in disturbing the dead.'

Jim went home. He put the bag containing the skull in the shed with his bicycle. All the same, he found himself wondering about the strange animal and, almost as if he was under some strange influence, he could not get the events out of his mind. That night he was unable to sleep and it was only after taking aspirin tablets that he was able to get any rest. He was to commence night shifts and he was not looking forward to that, not with the strange thoughts and worries crowding his mind.

At lunch time he went down to the pub, hoping to meet Ted. After two pints, he felt a bit better and Ted arrived. He did not say much but agreed that he had had queer thoughts and wondered whether they really were due to normal depression or the influence of the discovery. Both men felt better for the chat and company; they had discussed Dave, the vet's opinion and Ted asked, 'By the way, where is the skull now?' Jim told him and Ted said, 'I'll go and get it and put it back, then I'll cover it up until that museum chap comes.' Jim agreed.

Later that afternoon, Jim arrived at Ted's house. 'Did you take the bag out of the shed, Ted?' Ted looked surprised. 'No, I haven't had time,' he replied. Jim gasped. 'Well it's gone. Who's got it now?' Ted looked worried. Jim looked at his watch. 'I shall have to go Ted, I've got a lot to do before I go on shift. Perhaps it will turn up, it's only a skull.' Ted smiled. 'It can't do anyone any harm, so don't worry.'

That night, Jim was a bit happier and didn't think about the previous worries. He was busy and time was passing quickly. About 11 p.m. he was aware that the wind was getting up and was buffeting the wooden signalbox. The location of the box was remote, about one and a half miles from the village, but the line was busy and the box controlled the junction, so any signalman had to have his wits about him.

He was reading the daily newspaper and enjoying a cup of tea. The wind seemed to have dropped and everything seemed peaceful, when he was aware of a noise outside the box. Jim thought, 'Hello, is someone coming up to keep me company?'

and went to the door and looked out down the steps. The night was cool and a chill breeze made itself felt. He shivered and was about to turn and go inside, when he was aware of a shape. He peered and suddenly he saw a large form. He gasped. It was a large black dog with large orb-like eyes gazing up at him with a malevolent gaze. Then it bayed and Jim was stricken with terror. He leapt back into the cabin and locked the door. He sank into his chair and tried to compose himself. He fancied he could hear the thing moving about outside and he was glad that the door was locked. Whose dog was it? He had never seen it before. Luckily there was no more traffic on the line for the time being. He smoked incessantly until dawn lit the sky and then he cautiously looked around. He felt better. His relief came up the steps. 'Everything OK Jim?' Jim replied, 'Everything's fine.' and went home.

When he had had his breakfast, he went to the shed, opened the door and was nearly knocked out by the overpowering smell. 'Ugh,' gasped Jim. He began to tidy it up and look around for the plastic bag. No sign and he couldn't puzzle out where it could have gone. Then a thought. 'Uncle Albert often came to borrow various garden tools, perhaps he's got it. Yes, that's it. I'll go and ask him later.' After dinner, the sun shone and Jim cycled down to Uncle Albert's cottage, situated near the railway line, but the old man was not in. Jim looked in the windows to see if he was around, but nobody was there.

That night, the weather worsened, the wind blew up a gale, and it poured. Jim heard noises on the steps which he investigated – but no one was there. Then his next train was belled and he accepted it into his section, setting the signals etc. As the heavy diesel with its oil tank train slowly passed the box, he suddenly heard a noise outside. He looked out and there it was, the animal, the great yellow eyes and the epitome of evil in its gaze. He slammed the cabin door, only to hear the hurried application of train brakes. He could see the tail light of the oil train stopped! Something had happened. He threw the signals to danger and belled the message on and tore down the steps, his lamp and red flag in his hand. The guard of the oil train was running towards him. Jim shone his torch. The man's face was ashen. 'An old man,' he gasped. 'He threw himself under us, he must have done.' Jim ran to the scene. There under a wagon was the body of Uncle Albert and clutched in his hand was a plastic bag containing the splintered remains of an animal's skull . . .

Other Signalbox Mysteries

As previously mentioned in this book, signalboxes are the sort of railway infrastructure that, by their often remote location, are likely to have experiences of a supernatural nature and so it is no surprise that most signalmen have a tale of mystery and suspense that happened to friends of theirs. Not often the first person, always the third person but authentic all the same. After all, who are we to disbelieve these events which have occurred in the lonely box during a night shift when the wind wailed and buffeted the timber structure? The noises that pervaded the silence beggar description and the signalmen are, remember, level-headed, intelligent people who are hand picked to do a responsible, onerous job. All the same, signalmen can be a fund of unexpected tales and it is always interesting to hear their stories.

One box in Lincolnshire had the manifestations of a poltergeist or mischievous ghost apparent in the building but it was of a gentle nature and although it moved cups of tea and generally showed its mischievous attributes, it never hurt anybody and was not vicious or dangerous. No one knew much about it except that it was always there and so accepted. Pencils would hover in mid air and windows would open and shut, the door would open, the lights would go on and off.

The signalbox at Kirton Lindsey was the subject of an unexplained occurrence that was to baffle everyone for ever. Footsteps were heard coming up the steps, but no one ever appeared at the top of the steps. In the end it was accepted that this happened, but the only explanation offered was that the blasting in the nearby quarry for lime was to blame for the movement which suggested settlement. But that was a convenient guess and was it really the cause?

What, may we ask, caused the gate locking lever in Holton-le-Moor signalbox to ease itself out of the frame slowly but determinedly which, after thorough examination, provided no explanation as the rational cause?

Again, the explanation still defeats us for the reason why and how Claxby box, locked up and deserted, could give the 5–5–5 bell code to Market Rasen (the bell code for opening signalbox). These events are just a few of the unexplained happenings in signalboxes. Who are we to disbelieve them?

42

THE PLATELAYERS' HUT

During my researches for material to complete this book I have found that railwaymen in particular have been reluctant to allow their names to be used in a story, and have sometimes insisted that even the name of the location be changed; perhaps they fear leg pulling from their workmates!

The following tale was recalled by a retired plate-layer ganger who, as expected, has asked me to change his name for the purpose of this story. He was certainly helpful but did also request that the name of the location be altered too. 'It's between Louth and Willoughby but I'm not saying exactly or we'll have the whole world knowing!' And he would not be drawn any further, so now read on.

I was told of the story by a friend who knew the old platelayer who we shall call Fred. My friend Harry (a retired driver) fixed up a meeting at a local pub and we were able to talk and discuss the strange happenings.

Fred's story concerned a lineside hut used by the permanent way men otherwise known as platelayers and/or lengthmen. The hut was situated in a cutting on the track-bed of the old East Lincolnshire line that ran between Grimsby and Peterborough via Boston; we are talking about the southern section of this once busy line.

What was so special about an old sleeper-built hut used by men to keep their tools and equipment in one side and take shelter from the elements in the other?

The local children used to play in the cutting and had for a long time fancied the hut as a den or HQ for their games, but the hut was always locked by a large padlock securing a hasp that was red with rust but still secured the door. Some of the more irresponsible youths had tried to set fire to the building but somehow it did not catch and went out much to their disappointment! The windows had been broken years ago but the railway company had boarded the frames up with wooden battens which were very effective; they did however allow a view into the building and although the children could see in they were fascinated with the place and were happy playing in the cutting.

All was uneventful until one child came home and told his mother that he had met a 'funny old man' in the cutting, 'dressed in funny old clothes'. The child was emphatic, 'but he just went away, we looked for him but couldn't find him'. His mother reassured him, 'people often go down there with their dogs; don't worry, I'm sure he wouldn't hurt you, but perhaps you shouldn't go down there for a week or two, David.'

A few weeks later and quite unrelated to David's experience a group of children from a neighbouring village made their way over the fields for a walk with their dogs. They found the cutting and scrambled down the slopes of the cutting enjoying the freedom, the old hut looked interesting and they soon explored the area, that had reverted back to nature. The flora and fauna had restablished its claim to colonise the old trackbed.

The children found the hut door opened easily enough and cautiously they ventured in, the place smelt musty and stale but it fascinated them. The remains of a table and chair told of more ordered times, spiders were everywhere, a mouse scuttled across the dirt floor startling the younger children who squeaked with fear. Chattering excitedly the children tried to open the other part of the building but it was still padlocked securely, they could see a little through various cracks but there seemed to be nothing of interest in that part.

One more adventurous boy decided to explore the overgrown slope behind the hut and he was pushing his way through the undergrowth when he caught sight of a figure approaching the hut further down the slope; the boy was close enough to see that the figure was that of a tramp wearing tattered clothing and crowned with a battered trilby hat. When the figure looked up the boy was impressed by bright, blue eyes and a long nose but a kind expression. Taken by surprise and fear of the other the boy lost his balance and tumbled down the grassy bank towards the stranger but to the boy's incredulous gaze the figure melted into thin air.

The other children hearing the boy's cries ran to him and he told them what had happened, they searched the cutting and the area around the hut without success. The other children pulled his leg and generally teased him about what he had seen but the child strenuously defended his story; somehow the fun had gone out of the adventure and they decided to return home.

The other boy, David, was also puzzling about his experience in the cutting and had resolved to go back and try to find out if he had been dreaming; somehow he did not feel frightened but more determined to see the tramp and make friends with him. One night when his parents were out David returned to the scene; as expected everything was quiet not even a walker with a dog was passing through, David cautiously approached the old hut, he peered through a crack in the battens before going round to the door which to his surprise was ajar. Very slowly he entered the hut, there was no one there, no sign of life only cobwebs and neglect. As he turned he caught a glimpse of something go past the open door, he dashed outside in time to see the figure of the old tramp going towards the slope as if to climb up and away. David ran after the figure that was nearly at the top, almost over the lip of the cutting, the figure then looked round to face the boy and smiled, then to David's amazement disappeared into thin air.

The boy searched around the area but the man, or whatever had been a human, had gone leaving the boy bewildered and confused.

When he arrived home his parents had returned home and

he was able to tell them what had happened; their first reaction was one of anger at his disregard of their wishes but they were interested in his story. Afterwards the boy's father decided to consult the local policeman to ask his views about the affair.

A day or two later the policeman called and was told about the strange experiences. 'I think I remember a tale long ago about a similar matter,' he said. He rubbed his chin, 'Some years ago a platelayer named Jed Knighton opted out of the rat race and became what I suppose you'd call a tramp. He wandered about this neck of the woods and he was quite harmless, he was fond of children. Anyway he lived in the old hut after the railway was taken up, we didn't see much of him in the winter but when the spring came round he would appear again. Then one year, about, well I can't remember when, we missed him. Some of us worried and went looking for him, then one of Alf Wood's sons found him dead in the old pw hut, we think he died of a heart attack or so the doctor said. Not a mark on him so it must have been natural causes; anyway it would seem that he comes back to his old home or sort of stamping ground. I'd heard tales about some people having seen an old man down there but not for a long while, he wouldn't hurt anyone so your lad needn't be scared of him.'

Fred says that was the last sighting of the spirit of Jed Knighton so his soul found its peace at last.

43

A STRANGE EXPERIENCE
AT WALTON JUNCTION

It was during the summer months of 1968 that my father first began taking me to Walton Junction, Liverpool to see what must have been the very last of the steam trains thunder past at 7 o'clock.

I loved trains, but I could remember the mounting excitement that I felt, as we approached the path leading to the station, change suddenly and inexplicably to fear.

The path ran parallel to the lines and junction box northwards towards the station itself. The fear always came when I was about halfway down the path. There was a strange feel about the place as though somebody or something was watching. It always seemed to mar our visits. The eyes even seemed to watch me when, during the autumn, I often picked wild blackberries at the end of the platform.

One particular Easter, a beautiful day, I remember an overwhelming fear filling me with absolute terror as we stood outside the ticket office after returning from a journey. It was indescribable and I intensely disliked that spot ever since.

During the damp November evenings when the gas lamp flickered in the wind, nothing would convince me that danger wasn't lurking in the eerie shadows.

During the summer of 1975 I visited the station one day when we had nothing particular to do, with two friends. I was astonished when we began walking down the now weed-strewn path to feel a familiar feeling of fear and expectation.

Both my friends felt that there was something 'queer' about the place and we left quickly. A few weeks later we returned, this time with a third friend, a very level-headed girl. We told her nothing of our horrible experience. This time we settled in the deserted waiting room which was silent and cold.

After a very short time we all felt a horrible feeling of being watched and an intangible atmosphere of dread and doom. My third friend was very scared and wanted to go at once, feeling that we were in definite danger from something. We left as darkness was descending on that foreboding place and nothing could have made us stay or convinced us that there was not something awful waiting in the station.

Recently, I returned to Walton Junction with my children to get the train to Ormskirk. We used the same old path, and I was amazed to realise that without knowing it I had been hurrying my children along and constantly looking over my shoulder. I was convinced something was following us, though nothing was visible.

We paused on the small bridge which led to the ticket office, I looked at the now derelict railway cottages which stood silent, lost and forlorn. The feeling of fear had subsided somewhat and I remembered looking into the rubble-strewn backyards and thinking how sad it was that they were now in ruin, as last time I was at the station they were occupied. Suddenly, we all heard a loud bang from the back bedroom of the second cottage, as though a door had been slammed hard. It was a cold calm day with no wind.

We waited to see if anyone came out, maybe a cat or a dog, but everywhere was silent and still. There was so much rubbish and broken glass littered about anyway that it would have been difficult for anyone to climb out without making a lot of noise.

So we left and resumed our journey. The uncanny, oppressive atmosphere still hangs over that spot as it has done for over twenty years.

44

THE ISLE OF MAN,
THE RAMSEY MYSTERY

This story involves a youth hostel in the town of Ramsey in the Isle of Man whose narrow-gauge railway has brought pleasure and fascination to many people either as holiday makers or railway enthusiasts since the 1870s.

Let Mr J. Glasscock tell the story.

I can be reasonably precise about the date and time of the occurrence, it was at the Ramsey hostel and the time was 11.30pm in late July 1967 and I think it was a Wednesday.

1967 was the year that the Isle of Man Railway reopened and I was feeling very emotional about the whole affair, with good reason, as the idea of the Isle of Man without a railway was quite unthinkable. I did actually get over to work for them in 1968–70 and 1971, but this story I am referring to was in 1967 when I was just paying a visit and was given a bed for the night in the hostel. There are two things to note about Ramsey Station; first of all, its extension line, the harbour branch, had closed years before, and secondly, no engine was ever kept at the station overnight because the shed water supply had been disconnected.

So I, and the only other lad in the dormitory, who was also a railway enthusiast, were surprised and stunned to hear, just as we were slipping off to sleep, the sound of wagons being shunted in the station. These wagons had a different coupling system over in the island; the sound of I O M shunting is quite different from mainland shunting, you don't get the clunk of the links on a loose-coupled wagon but a delayed clank as the 'chopper' of one drops over the buffing plate of another. When you have listened to it many times as we had, you get to recognise the unique sound, it is absolutely unmistakable.

At first, we could only hear the wagons and we thought that it could be someone hand-shunting, but at this time of night? Also we couldn't understand why, since there were only three trains a day each way, and only the 11.50am arrival and the 4.05pm departure were ever heavy trains. We only knew for certain that there was something strange afoot when we heard the sounds of a train being marshalled and it started coming towards the hostel, what is more terrifying was that it was coming on a non-existent track! Had it been a real train the sound would have faded off towards the west - away from the hostel instead, and we could now hear the engine as well; it came towards the hostel over the non-existent harbour branch and clattered to a stop, perhaps at one of the wharves. And then we heard one final hiss of the safety valves and then silence.

There were seven people in our dormitory and I think five were awake; we all heard the mysterious sounds without any doubt but it appeared that none of the inhabitants of the other dormitories heard anything at all. We, of course, went outside to see if we could see anything, not really expecting to; there was nothing to suggest the passage of a train, just the cool night air and the distant sound of night life, nothing to prove or disprove the eerie sounds we had heard so clearly. Was it wishful thinking? Could I have been dreaming? I think not as four other unsolicited accounts verified my experience. We had been privy to a re-enactment of the movements of a former working on the old harbour branch, and although not frightened we were all very puzzled by the strange sequence of events.

45

ASHTON MOSS JUNCTION

There would appear to be a considerable number of strange events concerning signal boxes and their environs more so than other areas of unexplained activities. In spite of many attempts to allay fears and promotion of the normal working conditions by the railway authorities, signal boxes are rather emotive places and one doesn't have to have a very fertile imagination to get into the feeling of unease and expectancy.

However, a story, again entirely without explanation, concerns Ashton Moss Junction, but let Mr Ian McGill reveal the mystery.

This story concerns a location about $^3/_4$ mile west of Ashton-under-Lyme station where a freight-only line from Denton Junction on the Stockport to Stalybridge line bifurcates to join the Manchester to Huddersfield Trans Pennine route by way of west and east facing curves. The point of bifurcation at the southernmost point of the triangle is Ashton Moss South Junction, whilst the western and eastern points of convergence with the Manchester to Huddersfield line are known as Ashton Moss North Junction and OA & GB (Oldham Ashton & Guide Bridge Junctions) respectively.

My informant (who wishes to be anonymous but nevertheless truthful) had spent a short time in his early days as a signalman at OA & GB Junction Signal box. Whilst on duty one Saturday afternoon during the early part of 1975, he heard the sound of footsteps ascending the steps leading up to the box, then he became aware of the figure of a man about to enter the lobby or vestibule outside the door. Expecting the visitor to knock to gain admittance, the signalman walked towards the door to see what the visitor wanted. However, the anticipated knock never came and opening the door of the box he found the lobby silent and totally devoid of anyone, the strange visitor had vanished without trace. The signalman went down the steps to search for signs of the visitor but there was no one about. A complete mystery.

The brief glimpse the signalman gained of the stranger was not sufficient to give a good description except that he was male and he appeared to be carrying a bag. Was this the shade of a railwayman visiting his former workplace? Could he have been a signalman who met an unfortunate death and still haunts the place of his end? To continue:

The following Saturday afternoon, my informant was once again on duty when the light began to fade – he hated the short winter days; suddenly he heard a sound, a strange sound of movement below the box. He went to the top of the steps and looked around, he couldn't see anyone or anything untoward; he looked out of the window and he thought he saw a figure on or around the track. In the vicinity of a road bridge, which spanned the line near Ashton Moss South Junction, about 200 yards away to the south, the signalman at Ashton Moss North Junction box also became aware of someone out on the track whom he took to be trespassing. After conferring, the two signalmen decided to try and apprehend the person concerned, and after making sure that the control had been told of the situation and the boxes were safe to leave they walked towards each other, approaching the trespasser from opposite directions, so keeping him in view all the time and affording him little chance of escape. Nevertheless, on reaching the spot where they had seen a person loitering, there was no one to be seen.

I don't have to stress the danger of anyone moving about on a railway track; ignorance is no excuse for trespassing on railway property and the warning notices are always abundant, which

136

is the reason that the two men were so concerned, firstly for the person's safety and secondly for the risk of a collision with a train and the undoubted injuries that would result. The two men were not concerned with ghosts, only the safe operation of the signal box and its environs.

The person they sought had disappeared into thin air; it was only then did they puzzle and wonder if the dusk had conned them into imagining that they could be mistaken. I could understand one man imagining that he saw a person in the immediate area of the box but it is hard to believe that two level-headed signalmen could have been mistaken enough to be confused by the same phenomenon. My informant thinks that what he saw was genuine and was certain that someone was down there, his mate in the other box was equally sure that he too saw the figure. If any person had the authority to be in the vicinity he would be wearing a high visibility vest, as laid down in the Railway Regulations, it would be madness not to do so.

I am told that other people have had similar experiences but are not prepared to enlarge on their stories; perhaps they had seen a ghost of a long-gone railwayman who had worked in the area years ago and had come back to his earthly place of employment! The mystery remains and perhaps will never be solved, but one thing is for sure, those two signalmen were absolutely certain of what they had seen and were unshakeable in their beliefs.

46

LYONSHALL STATION

The village of Lyonshall in Herefordshire near the Welsh borders was provided with a station by the Great Western Railway; this station had a somewhat chequered history and a rather inconsistent patronage.

The small railway outpost had the Indian sign on it when closure came entirely on 1 January 1917 in the midst of World War I. However, some five years later the GWR had a change of heart and decided to reopen the station to goods traffic on 18 September 1922. Subsequent re-opening to passengers on 11 December 1922 heralded a new era for the station and trade seemed to have awakened to the transport needs of the community.

But again in a wartime emergency, when one would imagine that *all* railway stations would be needed during a war, the axe fell again on Lyonshall Station and it was closed to all traffic on 1 July 1940 and abandoned.

My correspondent, Mr Glasscock of Braintree, Essex, has a very strange tale to tell that even today has no logical explanation.

During the hot summer of 1959, on a particularly heavy and sultry day and following morning, I and a friend visited Lyonshall Station. We were on a cycling holiday and me being very interested in railways generally, liked looking over old stations.

Lyonshall Station was, and I very much doubt that any trace

of it remains today, in a very dangerous condition. The bridge had been removed but the wooden platform and building were visible from the road below; there was a roofed stairway leading to platform level, every step was either missing or rotten, so the bottom of the staircase was made completely inaccessible with barbed wire criss-crossed right up to the old roof beam. Over the years brambles had spread in all directions and had wound round the barbed wire, so it would have taken an axe or some other sharp tool to have gained entry, one certainly couldn't have reached the top of the stairway at all.

The general condition was extremely dangerous and one could expect difficulty in trying to gain any access as the stairway was so derelict.

I remarked to my friend, 'You'd have to wait for a long time to get a train from here,' he smiled and we both set off for the youth hostel down the road. I believe that it is closed now.

In the morning, though our route lay the other way, I insisted on going back to the old station for one more look. It seemed sad to see the old place decaying, uncared for and neglected. I was convinced that something had happened in our absence; something had indeed happened – it had rained hard during the night and early morning – which was strange for that summer when we had a period of almost drought conditions. Anyway the steps that remained, and there weren't many of them, were still damp since the roof of the stairway was as rotten as everything else. But so clearly visible and definitely new since the previous evening was a set of footprints, and looking around, a set of tracks, small hob-nailed boot tracks going up the staircase to the top and not coming down. I shuddered, the very thought of anyone being so foolish baffled me, the steps were so rotten that it wouldn't have taken any weight to have snapped them and sent anyone plunging down causing a bad injury.

The prints were about my own size, $6^1/_2$ and my own guess for what it is worth, since, as a cadet I did own a pair of hob-nails, is that my own almost religious love of country railways had revealed a kind of secular stigmatic effect. My friend was most unimpressed, he had seen the footprints but shrugged his shoulders and suggested that we move on. However, the mystery remains and I will never forget it and will always puzzle over the mysterious footprints that defied all the obstacles, or did they?

47

THE SCENT OF THE ROSE

Charlotte Campbell was more than delighted to have received a reply to her letter for the position of children's nanny which she had seen advertised in *The Times*. She hoped for a reply, but dared not hope too much; she imagined that the Hon Mrs Anderson-Hunt would have had many replies and perhaps ladies with experience would be far more preferable to a young comparatively inexperienced girl like her. But in 1906 it was the accepted procedure to reply to letters and Charlotte was so excited at the invitation to visit Winstable Hall for an interview.

The Hon Mrs Anderson-Hunt had sent a crisp 10s note for her train fare and expenses, and that sum would adequately cover those. Charlotte couldn't contain her delight.

Never having been more than ten miles from her parents, home in her nineteen years the prospect of a fifty-mile train journey seemed like an adventure and she would travel alone, but maybe she would meet some handsome young man! She smiled at the thought; the next seven days to the interview seemed almost endless in the long hot summer of 1906.

Charlotte woke very early on 21 September, giving herself plenty of time to make the very best of herself, putting on her Sunday best dress and bonnet. Her heart was beating much faster as she approached the railway station, she offered her 10s note to the booking clerk and received her return ticket to Wiltham which was the nearest station to Winstable Hall.

There according to her letter a trap would be waiting to convey her to the Hall.

Charlotte walked slowly onto the platform and waited for her train to pull in. Soon a plume of smoke heralded its arrival and Charlotte was held in awe as the gleaming locomotive hauled the immaculate rake of teak coaches into the station. The engine stopped alongside her and a young man with blond hair and a cheery smile jumped down. 'Hello,' he greeted. She smiled demurely. 'How far are you going?' Charlotte replied that she was going to Wiltham and she had an important interview. The young man said he would tell her when to get off and then busied himself with an oilcan among the driving wheels.

Charlotte stepped into the first compartment and sat down, the station was now a hive of activity, Charlotte leaned out of the window and watched the guard's van being loaded up with milk churns, sacks of mail, and boxes of red roses. The other passengers had found their seats, the whistle blew, and the young fireman leaned over the door and handed Charlotte a single red rose. Smiling, Charlotte thanked him. 'I'm Albert,' he smiled.

It was not a long journey and as the sun was shining it was a very pleasant one. Eventually the train pulled into Wiltham and Albert leapt down and opened the carriage door, taking Charlotte's hand and helping her down. 'There we are, I hope you get the post!' Charlotte thanked him and passed through the barrier into the station yard where a uniformed coachman was waiting with a trim little gig to take her to meet the Hon Mrs Anderson-Hunt.

Charlotte did get the position of nanny and often travelled on the same train home on her days off, always in the first compartment behind the tender and always hoping that she would see Albert, which she often did and she leaned out of the window to talk to him when the train stopped in the stations.

It was over a year before Charlotte was allowed to take her charge, a little boy called Edward, home with her to meet her family on her day off. It was a very sunny day and it was made all the more complete by Albert being on duty on the return journey. He had jumped down to open the carriage door for her and Charlotte and the child made to get in. Albert was talking to them as they waited to leave, and the boy had a large rubber ball that he would insist on throwing about in the compartment. Charlotte, her eyes on Albert who was taking her attention, asked him rather half-heartedly to desist, but the boy threw the ball out of the window. It hit the platform fence and ran under the carriage; as quick as a flash the boy darted past Charlotte and Albert and tried to look for it under the wheels. As Charlotte scrambled out of the carriage the boy was halfway under the carriage; almost beside herself, Charlotte and Albert tried to haul him up. The driver had seen the green flag and had opened the regulator to ease forward, yelling at Albert to come on. By this time Charlotte was halfway under the carriage with Albert trying to help her. The boy had got jammed and couldn't get out. The train eased forward, the driver unaware of the panic. Charlotte screamed, the driver panicked, his hand still on the regulator. Albert leapt onto the footplate, missed his footing and grabbed the regulator to stop himself falling; the train moved forward dragging the nanny and child under the wheels. Nothing could save them, the wheels had passed over them and life had gone.

But that was not the end of this sad story, nor of the nanny and child who died so horribly.

Many people have seen Charlotte waiting for Albert, or her ghost who refuses to leave this station. Albert was so distressed by the whole affair that he applied for another post further away from the scene of the tragedy.

But sightings of the young lady continued and the curious point was that people used to say that in the first compartment next to the tender there would often be the strong scent of roses.

After a while the station returned to normal, Charlotte hadn't been seen for some time, and Albert had been killed in World War I so all three participants in the awful tragedy had gone for ever, or had they?

Just before the outbreak of World War II a long passenger train was in the station taking water. The driver was oiling an axle box when he turned round to see the trim figure of a young lady with a small boy near the first compartment of the carriage next to the tender. He made as if to talk to them when they melted before his very eyes; he couldn't believe it and as the guard approached he told him what he had seen. The guard smiled, 'It's Charlotte and the boy, we've seen her on many occasions. By the way, can you smell that lovely scent of roses?'

48

THE FURNESS RAILWAY MYSTERY

I am very grateful to Mr R. R. Mester for the following story of strange happenings on a long abandoned stretch of railway between Goldmire Junction and Millwood Junction on the original line of the Furness Railway.

My correspondent's earliest and most vivid recollection of a haunted railway line dates from childhood memories of some sixty years ago and refers to the short length of line between Goldmire Junction and Millwood Junction on the old Furness Railway in the area of Dalton-in-Furness.

Opened in 1846 this section had been early superseded and closed and in the time of Mr Mester's childhood comprised only an overgrown formation. There were many trees and shrubs about so visibility was rather restricted, a footpath crossed both railway and stream just below Millwood, and there was a large detached residence. It was a creepy spot with a strong pungent smell of garlic and there was always a feeling of tension and foreboding.

Frequently and for no apparent reason, there would be a chilling burst of wind and a roar as of a passing train. In the gloaming it was possible to glimpse passing lights identical to those of a carriage in a moving train, altogether it was an eerie happening – crossing a long-abandoned railway in the Vale of Nightshade!

Down in the Vale lay the ruins of Furness Abbey – founded by one king (Stephen) and destroyed by another king, Henry

VIII, at the Dissolution of the Monasteries. The roar was held by some to be that of the dispossessed and not a train at all. My fears were shared by youthful friends and even adult relatives at times seemed to 'chivvy' us along as if they too expected the ghost train to rush by. Some seemed quite certain of a mystery train – one they heard that came and vanished but was never recognised.

Years later it seemed reasonable to identify the ghost train with nearby trains on well concealed tracks linking Dalton-in-Furness with Askam-in-Furness and Barrow-in-Furness respectively, but this explanation did not entirely remove the doubts and fears experienced even in retrospect.

Maybe there was a mystery train of sorts deriving from some forgotten tale in an area served early by rail linking with wild and remote sea shores. Whatever the explanation, for some of us there was always a sense of fear in this secluded spot and that moreover linked to a train.

Perhaps it was no more than old *Coppernob*, Furness Railway No 3, built in 1846 and resident in those school days in its great glass case outside Barrow Central Station, taking a turn over its old hunting grounds . . .

49

THE SPIRIT ENTITY

I have called this story the Spirit Entity because it illustrates the fact that earthbound factions are still very active, and making their presence felt in so many unexpected ways. I am indebted to my correspondent Mrs D. M. Ross for this compelling tale.

Mrs Ross was one of six senior citizens travelling between Glasgow and Paisley in a DMU; they were in the rear carriage with the brake unit in the centre. The train braked to a shuddering halt at the Paisley signal box where it remained for the next thirty minutes whilst the driver and guard proceeded to examine the underside and topside of the train. Eventually the guard climbed aboard and entered Mrs Ross's carriage and demanded to know who had pulled the communication cord which none of the passengers could see from their seated position. When the guard was told that no one had moved from their seats he became very worried because he said he had to make out a report to British Rail as to the cause of the delay and he then said, 'I'll have to put it down to person or persons unknown'. To which one lady said, 'That would be a complete lie, have you never heard of a Spirit Entity?'

The central position of the brake section prevented anyone moving along the train without being noticed, the guard agreed to this point. It did not solve his problem but the poor fellow had to make out his report and he had to find some element of evidence and so far he hadn't got much to write down. How the poor fellow finally got his report together I do not know but I doubt that even he didn't realise that he was dealing with a supernatural force that did what it liked when it liked.

Mrs Ross tells me that she later discovered that several years earlier near Paisley signal box two trains had collided with loss of life. My informant tells me that she feels sure that the earlier event is still 'earthbound' and repeated the action. I imagine that the frustrated passengers would not be amused if they realised that the delay was caused by a restless spirit but the report of the accident can be checked in British Rail's archives.

So this strange occasion and its tragic precedent can be the work of the past or present spirit entity . . .

50

YARWELL TUNNEL

I am very grateful to Mr H. E. Caunt, the Public Relations Officer for the Nene Valley Railway in Cambridgeshire, who kindly sent me details of the strange happenings concerning Yarwell Tunnel.

During the construction of the Blisworth to Peterborough branch line of the old London & Birmingham Railway in 1845, the engineer and surveyor of the route, one Robert Stephenson, being faced with a hilly terrain near to the villages of Yarwell and Wansford decided to tunnel through as a cutting was not practicable at that time.

Hence gangs of navvies (mainly Irish) were set to work on the task of excavation and works; they lived in mud huts, huts which would only offer the most primitive shelter from the elements. Kilns were established to manufacture the bricks used to line the tunnel (approximately one million were made), and the clay used came by barges on the nearby Nene. Weekends were a particularly troublesome time, drunkenness and fighting was a real problem and special police had to be drafted in to take charge. It was reported at the time that ten or more navvies met their death fighting and falling from scaffolding as this tunnel is unusually high and was built to accommodate double tracks.

The late Mr Walter Gilbey used to tell of many strange happenings during maintenance work in the tunnel; mysterious noises, agonising cries and sounds of men fighting. Hammers

149

and shovels used to disappear without trace, a newly laid stretch of track was found the following morning with all the wooden keys on the tunnel side all knocked out. Sabotage was suspected but after a thorough investigation was never proved.

On another occasion some gangers had to jump for their lives as a freight train suddenly entered the tunnel without any warning from the lookout men at either end of the tunnel. As soon as the train had cleared the tunnel the gangers found one of the lookout men lying unconscious by the side of the track. On reviving him the man told the head ganger that he had been struck by a blow at the back of the head yet medical evidence revealed no sign of injury, furthermore his whistle, flags, and lamp were never found.

Another strange happening concerns a one-time station master at Wansford Station who had a pet cat called Snowy which used to follow him everywhere. One late autumn afternoon Snowy failed to turn up for his meal, so his master went out to look for him. Unfortunately the station master was rather deaf and he failed to hear an approaching train in the inky darkness of the tunnel and he was struck down and killed. Snowy was never seen again.

Yet on many occasions a greyish-white cat has been seen crying piteously entering the tunnel never to reappear; none of the local cats are like Snowy, being either black, black-and-white, ginger or tortoiseshell!

So Yarwell Tunnel has its mysterious and macabre secrets, sharing with some these facets and leaving an indelible memory in the mind.

51

BRIDGE 173

Bridge 173 was an agricultural occupation bridge spanning a deep railway cutting and was used by the local farmer to give access to both big lineside fields.

It was a very sound brick structure and had been built about 1868 but it had the notorious reputation of being called 'Lover's Leap', no doubt due to the fact that several suicide attempts had been made from its high parapet, most of them fatal.

One particular night, young John Armitage, a very junior passed engine cleaner had no notion of the bridge's notoriety. He had just fired up and sat down to rest. His mate, driver Sam Webster, gave him a smile of approval and said, 'Good lad, young John, now put your injector on, shut it off when you've got nearly a full "glass", then have a few minutes. I'll tell you when to fire up again just before we go up the bank.' Young John did as he was told. This was his first mainline trip and he was grateful to Sam for his advice and also for him taking him on this trip.

The shed running foreman had asked Sam if he would take young John as there was no one available at the time. He explained that although the lad had not been on the mainline before, he was a good, reliable and sensible lad. Sam, without any hesitation had agreed knowing that to wait for the first available fireman would delay his train's departure. Young John had been delighted. He had done a reasonable amount of pilot work, firing for some of the older shunt link drivers and had also fired on the local 'pick-up', but this at last was the real thing.

So far, driver Sam Webster was pleased with his young mate's performance and had noted with approval how he used his firing shovel to spread the coal systematically round the firebox and his ability to fire up through the firehole door trap without having to open the door. With a little bit more experience and confidence, he would undoubtedly make a 'good 'un'.

Young John, seated on his cabside fireman's seat, looked interestedly about him. Poking his head out from the cab, to get a little cooling draught, he noticed that they were about to enter a long deep cutting and marvelled at the way the cutting must have been cut through almost solid rock. The track took a right hand curve and for the first time he saw the bridge standing high above the track. Approaching the bridge, he had a shock. Although it was getting dusk, he was certain that he had seen someone or something fall from the bridge.

Frozen with shock, momentarily, he recovered his scattered wits and shouted, 'Sam, stop; someone's jumped off the bridge.' Sam acted quickly. As a mainline driver, his reflexes were excellent. Smartly closing the regulator, he made a partial application of the steam brake, paused, released it, paused once again, then when he heard the wagon buffers face up, he made a full brake application. He knew of course that he would never be able to halt the train before it reached the bridge and he had his guard's safety to think about. If he had made a full brake application, his guard, Gerry Briggs, would have been thrown from one end of the brakevan to the other with a possible resultant injury.

As the train slowed down, Sam came over to the fireman's side and looked out and seeing nothing, suddenly realised the legend of the bridge. He looked at young John, now white and shaken with the shock. 'Don't worry, young John,' he said, to comfort and reassure him. 'You kept a good lookout.' As the train slowed to a halt, he remembered other drivers, mostly some of the 'old hands', talk about Bridge 173 and how some of them joked about the 'strange sightings' near it.

With the train stopping about a train's length beyond the bridge, he knew that he would have to walk back and explain to Gerry and have a look. 'Stop on the engine, John,' he said. 'I'll go back and have a look and see the guard.' Walking back to the end of the train, he found the guard standing on the track beside his brakevan. 'What's up then, Sam?' he asked. 'Anything wrong with the engine?' 'No,' Sam said. 'My mate thought he saw something or someone fall off the bridge.'

The guard climbed up into his brakevan, to return with a can of detonators in case he had to protect the train. 'Come on then, Sam, let's have a look.' Reaching the bridge, they had a good look round but found nothing. 'Bloody bridge,' Gerry said, 'the last time this happened was about five years ago, when Jack Thompson saw something. Do you remember everybody laughed about it? Come on, Sam, let's get going. If we get a move on, we'll make the time up. I don't think we should report it, do you?' 'Not so likely,' Sam agreed. 'I'll tell young John not to say anything.' Quickly they returned to the train and once more started off. On the move once again, Sam told his young fireman all about the legend of the bridge. 'Will you have to report it?' John asked. 'Not so bloody likely,' Sam said. 'If I tell anyone that we stopped to look for a ghost, they'll laugh at me, and if I was you, I wouldn't tell your mates either. Just tell them that you know now where Bridge 173 is.'

52

THE BARMAN'S STORY –
A SEQUEL TO BRIDGE 173

It was a sunny autumn afternoon in 1963 as John and Mary Briggs were walking along a disused trackbed in the Westcountry with their two Jack Russell terriers, Tina and Spot, who were enjoying their walk as much as their owners. There was so much to sniff at and they had already found two rabbits and had aroused a flock of partridges.

When they reached the approach to what appeared to be a long deep cutting, Mary stopped. 'Let's go back, I think we've gone far enough and it looks dark and spooky.' Was it a woman's intuition? The two dogs settled the matter, racing on ahead. John looked at his watch, 'Come on Mary, we can go on for another ten minutes and I'd like to find out what is around that bend.' So reluctantly she followed her husband through the cutting. Eventually they saw ahead of them the bridge standing high and spanning the valley; red crumbling brick it stood, carrying a farm road and seldom used by anyone else. As they drew nearer John could just make out a plate on which the number 173 was discernible.

Suddenly, the dogs who were sniffing this exciting new country stopped; ears raised, hair rising on their necks, they backed slowly towards John and Mary, then they howled and turned and ran back through the cutting, leaving John and Mary puzzled and a bit frightened. Mary shuddered 'I don't like this place, it seems sad and depressing, don't you think it's turned cold?' John had to agree, he too felt a bit uneasy and scared but didn't want to show his fear to Mary. 'OK, let's go back to the hotel, then we'll have a nice cup of tea.' Mary smiled and kissed him.

Later that evening when they were seated comfortably in the bar Mary brought up the subject of the eerie feeling in the cutting; they agreed it had been a most disturbing experience and that there must be some explanation. John said 'I'll ask the barman if he knows anything about it.' Steve, the barman, was polishing a glass as John approached the bar. 'NoW sir, what can I get you?' he asked. John ordered a pint of bitter and a sweet martini. While Steve was busying himself John asked him about the bridge and the strange feeling in the cutting. Steve placed the drinks on the counter, 'There we are, sir, that will be . . .' After the till drawer closed, he turned and said, 'Bridge 173 sir? It's haunted, and I would keep well away from it. It's bad news around here sir, and the bridge seems to attract suicides. They used to come here, yes, to this hotel to spend their last nights before they went to that bridge to hurl themselves off, sometimes in front of a train; but now the line has gone and the track removed we don't get so many nuts coming to end their days. Now only Alf Hurst, he farms the land either side of the cutting, uses it to get across but even Alf doesn't like it. The wind always blows cold in that cutting and across the old bridge.'

John listened, fascinated with Steve's story. 'Mary and I took our dogs down there this afternoon and I must admit we didn't like it, Mary was quite frightened. We won't go again I can assure you.' Steve nodded, 'Very wise sir, they used to call the spot under the bridge, "Lover's Leap". It's a brooding, desolate place that.' Mary came over to the bar, on that the two men stopped talking and smiled at her. 'Can I have my drink, it seems as if you two will talk all night,' she said. 'Let's go and sit down, dear,' she said to her husband. She took his arm, 'Just a minute sir,' said Steve. Mary took her drink to her seat and prepared to wait again. 'One thing that might interest you, last year our manager jumped from that bridge and broke his neck . . .'

53

THE OLD LOCO SHED

The old loco shed stood gaunt, derelict and roofless, amidst the mounds of brick rubble and refuse surrounding it. The once busy shed, now with the skeletal, unclad girders of its roof standing stark against the darkening sky, was just a ghost of its former self. As it was soon to be finally and completely demolished, I took the first opportunity of looking round and about the old shed to see if I could find something, anything, of interest relating to the depot to add to my growing collection of 'Railwayana'.

The loco shed had many sentimental memories for me as my late father had been a mainline driver there many years ago before the branch line, with its four stations, marshalling sidings, loco shed and workshops closed, shortly after the closure of the two adjacent collieries. The branch line had survived for a few years as a single line until its final demise.

As I passed what had been the marshalling yard and sidings, I glanced at the rows of rusting buffer stops and rotting wooden buffer beams, and conjured up a picture of its lines of laden coal wagons waiting to be despatched and the coal empties waiting to be taken to the collieries to be filled. It was a cold, wet, typically late autumnal afternoon as I walked along the old trackbed, avoiding the many puddles of murky rainwater on my way. I stopped momentarily to look at the old 'cenotaph' or what remained of it. The once modern coaling plant was now just a mass of huge broken lumps of concrete. Would there be anything collectable there, I wondered. I decided against looking into the tumbledown wooden hut that had once housed the coal hopper controls. The rotting wooden walkway looked too perilous to risk any injury so I continued on my way to the shed, now some seventy or eighty yards away. I stopped about twenty yards away from the shed, appalled at the scene of utter desolation and neglect. One of the shed's huge, wooden doors, the only survivor, hung crazily, on one rusting hinge, swaying slightly in the stiffening breeze. Continuing on my way, I saw that the outer and inner ash pits were filled with rubble and rubbish of every kind. What an inglorious end to what had once been a busy loco shed that had been the scene of so much activity in its heyday. Reaching the shed, I stepped over several mounds of brick and other rubble and went inside, looking carefully at the wet streaked brick walls searching for anything that could be identifiable with the depot. One of the rusting iron pipes fastened to the shed wall and apparently coming from what remained of the old boilerhouse inside, had a plate affixed to it, near the stump of what must have been a water stop valve.

It could be of interest, so taking a piece of cotton waste out of my pocket, I cleaned the accumulated filth off it, only to discover that on it was stamped ON–OFF. However, as it was brass, I decided that it was collectable. It was something at least. Taking the roll of tools out of my stout and well travelled haversack, I unscrewed the plate with only a little difficulty and put it into the haversack. I had got one souvenir and if not identifiable with the shed, at least I knew where it had come from. Walking further into the shed, I paused and looked around wondering how many times my old father must have walked through it. Then, on an impulse, I retraced my steps following the run of the old water washout pipes until I found myself in the remains of what must have been the old boilerhouse. It was there that I made my one and only good find, not of course taking into account the brass washout pipe plate. I saw a corner of what looked like a rusted iron plate protruding from a pile of brick rubble. Eagerly I set about to free it from its rubble prison. It took me about three or four minutes to rescue it and I looked at my 'prize'. Cleaning the muck off it I was delighted with my discovery. It read, 'LNWR–BOILERHOUSE–PRIVATE', and must have come off the boilerhouse door. It was not too big or cumbersome to take away so I packed it up in my stout old haversack and stepping out of the ruins of the boilerhouse, returned to the shed. It was getting dark and the wind had freshened, the rain gusting through the length of the shed so I decided that it was time to pack up and head for the nearest hospitable pub where I had been told I would be able to get a good meal of hot pie and peas. Dad had often spoken about the Railway Hotel just across the road from what remained of the station, and how he used to play the battered old piano and have a sing-song with his pals. Perhaps I would be able to conjure up his image while indulging myself with my pie and peas and a pint. On my way out of the shed, I suddenly realised that I was not on my own. There, walking down the middle of the shed in the gloom, I espied a dark blue-clad figure wearing what appeared to be what Dad used to call a 'steamraiser', a shiny topped peaked cap. The figure walked slowly down the shed. I was unable to see his face but as it was getting dark, I was not surprised. I was just about to speak when suddenly, abruptly, the figure disappeared. Had it been a figment of imagination, brought about with the increasing gloom, and the aura of the surrounding dereliction? No, I knew that I had seen someone, or something. I had never believed in ghosts but what I had seen was unaccountable. Suddenly, I heard a loud crash near me, scaring me out of my wits. The old shed door hanging on one rusted hinge, would swing no more and had crashed to the floor. It was enough for me, the last straw. I had seen and heard enough. Already startled by the apparition, the crashing down of the big heavy door completely unnerved me.

I ran out of the shed not looking back, raced across the old marshalling yard, out of the tumbledown gateway of the station, across the road and into the brightly lit warmth of the Railway Hotel bar. Faces looked strangely at me as I burst abruptly into the bar room. One old chap said, 'What's up lad, tha' looks as if tha's seen a ghost!' After getting my breath, I said, 'I think I have'. One kindly old chap stood up and said, 'Come on mate, sit down here, I'll get you a pint then you can tell us your story.' As I sat down, one old boy seated next to me said, 'Have you been walking on the old trackbed then?' 'Yes,' I replied. Another said, 'I bet you've been into the loco shed.' 'Yes,' I said. 'How did you know?' 'Tha's not first one to get a shock there mate,' he answered. 'What did you see then?' I then told them about the apparition, how I had seen someone walking down the shed and then suddenly disappearing. The kindly old chap who gave up his seat for me brought me my pint saying 'Drink this mate, you'll feel better when tha's supped that.' While I gratefully sipped my pint, they told me the story. Several people apart from myself had seen the 'loco apparition'. Between them, my new-found friends told me the story.

While the branch line and the loco shed was working, a driver from the shed had unfortunately failed the railway doctor with defective colour vision and as a result had been relegated to fire-lighting and steam-raising duties. He used to come in here regularly for a pint, they said. The chap who had been kind enough to get me my pint said, 'I was only a young chap at the time but I remember him well. Fred Grisenthwaite were his name. He were never the same when he came off mainline. It was a pity too about his accident as if he hadn't had enough bad luck.' 'What happened then?' I asked. 'He were firin' up and steamin' an engine when it happened. A tube burst and the blow back threw him back against the tender end. He must have hit his head for it killed him. At the time we said "poor old Fred, we'll never see him again." We haven't, but others have, including you now evidently.' I had by now recovered my scattered senses and after finishing off my enjoyable meal of pie and peas and my second pint, I thanked my kind new-found friends and left the hospitable Railway bar to walk back down to where my trusty old Morris Minor was parked. It had without doubt been a day to remember and now whenever I look at my LNWR Boilerhouse Private plate, I think of poor unfortunate Fred Grisenthwaite and his tragic demise, and then recall the Railway Hotel bar room and the kind friends I met that night.

54

GLASGOW UNDERGROUND
HAUNTINGS!

The Glasgow underground railway system like the London underground counterpart has some very strange and totally unexplained events. The sceptics will scoff as usual but my informants are adamant in their accounts of the happenings.

The Glasgow system runs in a circle beneath the city centre and is narrow gauge 4ft; it serves a pressing transport need. It also plays host to a number of strange, ghostly occurrences according to a book *I belong to Glasgow* by Bill Hamilton and Gordon Carsely, from which I am most obliged for the information.

The aforementioned book was written before the system closed for extensive modernisation and I have no further information (in spite of research) that any more unexplained events have occurred.

In the old days there was no physical access from the running lines to Govan car sheds and workshops, so stock was only brought out of the tunnels for repair and maintenance, which necessitated lifting the vehicles bodily off the track and up through pits into the workshops by means of a large overhead crane. At night after close of the service it was the practice to stable the empty trains end to end on the running lines in the tunnels on each side of the shed car pits, the end doors of each vehicle opened to permit ready exit of passengers in the event of an emergency, and to allow access to the lines of stabled trains by cleaners and others whose nocturnal duties took them into the subway tunnels.

On one occasion a team of five men went down into the tunnels for which purpose they had to pass through the line of empty stabled cars. On reaching the last train they found a colleague talking to a middle-aged man dressed in a light-coloured rain coat and flat cap who was assumed to have been overcarried on the last train after going out of service at Capland Road Station. The stranger was led back through the empty trains to the car shed pits where he could gain access to the street. Looking back at regular intervals to see if the stranger was following, eventually they reached the access to the street but the guide was astonished to find the man had vanished into thin air. The men went back and searched the trains but the man had disappeared; all the men agreed the man had been there, they had all seen him, they were all completely baffled.

Govan car sheds were reputedly haunted by a figure which was seen from time to time in a driving compartment of a car but on investigation the figure had disappeared and was nowhere to be found; the cab was empty yet strangely cold! Cleaners working in the tunnels between Kelvinbridge and Hillhead Stations used to report hearing disembodied voices of women singing.

An accident in 1922 is believed to be the explanation for the appearance of the 'Grey Lady' whose ghostly form has been reported in the tunnel near Shields Road Station. In that year a lady and a little girl (presumably the daughter) fell from an otherwise deserted station platform into the path of an oncoming train; the station master on seeing the incident attempted to rescue them both but was only able to save the girl.

Two maintenance gangs who were working one night some distance apart on a section of track noticed a mysterious light between them but despite searching the area nothing could be found to explain the phenomenon. Finally, at around 3am one Sunday in 1967 pump man, Willie Baxter, was detailed to go through the tunnels from St Enochs to Bridge Street Station where he was to attend to a tank located beneath the stairs. After walking for some time, having covered about half the distance between the two stations, Willie became aware of a steady, yet rather unnerving sound just ahead as if someone was hammering the rails. The ganger, whose section this was and who might therefore have been responsible, had passed through some ninety minutes earlier. Willie Baxter was gripped by fear, he didn't understand it, he hated the dark tunnels, he stopped walking and the noise stopped; by now Willie was probably near the point where the tunnels passed under the River Clyde and it was said that it was possible to hear the sound of a ship's propeller whenever a vessel passed overhead. However, Willie was certain that this could not account for the strange noise, so he continued, only to find the noise started again even louder. That was it! He'd had enough, he turned and ran for his life back to St Enochs and the fresh air.

Later discussing the experience with his workmates the reaction was divided, some voiced complete disbelief, some agreed as they too had had similar experiences, others just nodded agreement with Willie. I am told that there have been further incidents since the system reopened but so far nobody has come along with any details.

My own belief is that tunnels are very emotive places and if one is susceptible to paranormal events a tunnel is just the sort of place for it to happen.

55

THE MYSTERY CHILDREN
AT CHARFIELD

The quiet Gloucestershire village of Charfield was on the main line of the LMS, situated between Gloucester and Bristol. The local Station served the surrounding community and carried a fair amount of passenger and freight traffic. The village hit the headlines, however, in a tragic way when an accident and fire happened on 13 October 1928.

The driver of the 10pm LMS passenger and mail train seemingly overran a home signal at danger and plunged into the rear of the 9.15pm OxlEY Sidings to Bristol GWR fitted goods before finally colliding with another freight, the 4.45 Westerleigh to Gloucester empties, that was passing on the opposite line.

Interlocking would have prevented the signalman putting the signals for the express at 'CLEAR' yet it is strange that although both footplatemen on the express admitted not having seen the home signal on the approach to Charfield both men were equally emphatic that they had seen the proceeding distant signal and they said it was showing a green light and in the clear position. Immediately following the accident it was discovered that the instrument in Charfield box bore this out and investigation showed that the distant arm was slightly inclined due to debris in the signal wire but not sufficient to show a green light through the spectacle plate.

It is strange therefore that the signal box instruments revealed it as clear, the signal must have been at green, or had a heavy weight been lying across the signal wire? Or again we ask, had the signal been tampered with? The footplatemen had nothing to gain by lying about the position of the distant signal when they admitted not seeing the home signal at all.

The mystery therefore, remains, but it is not the only mystery attached to the Charfield disaster, indeed the one which most concerns us in the context of the strange and uncanny is the riddle of the unclaimed bodies.

Fifteen lives were lost in the accident and the ensuing fire which raged for twelve hours. Two of the dead were children, a girl aged about eight or nine and a boy of about eleven years, they were travelling together, but otherwise unaccompanied. It was alleged that at first the railway company denied that they had been travelling on the train at all, and it was indeed suggested that the two children were chance victims of the holocaust and they happened to be wandering by the railway at the time. However, the evidence of the fireman who was on the footplate of the engine that was hauling the express disproved the allegations of the railway company, for he had seen them together on the train after it had arrived at Birmingham New Street Station around 2.30 when the children had waved at him. He subsequently saw them laughing and talking with the guard before the train left Birmingham and described both youngsters as well dressed; the boy was wearing a school uniform of yellow and brown with cap to match and scarf. Anything else the guard may have remembered is of no value for he was killed in the crash.

In the aftermath of the accident the bodies of the two children were recovered from the wreckage and laid beside the track with the other bodies of the tragedy, but their charred remains were beyond recognition and were never claimed nor was any connection established between them and the other passengers, and in consequence the two children were never identified.

Most of the victims were buried in the village churchyard of St James where the LMS erected a memorial with the names of those laid to rest there. The base of the memorial is inscribed with ten names and the emotive words 'Two Unknown'.

There is even some doubt in some quarters as to whether in fact the unfortunate children were interred at Charfield, for it was said that an Army vehicle was noticed briefly at the scene of the accident, and it has been suggested that some of the remains, possibly those of the children, were removed amid the general confusion.

Someone, somewhere must have been concerned for and worried about these unfortunate children and found their absence odd; surely too, someone must have paid their fare and seen them off on their journey. It is extremely likely, also, that someone was waiting for them at their intended destination.

56

THE MYSTERIES

OF BLEA MOOR TUNNEL

Talk to many a railwayman about the Blea Moor Tunnel and you will find either a spontaneous reaction of a flow of stories or complete and total silence. This bore has a very unpleasant reputation and the local people don't like going near the place at night especially as the rail traffic today has been considerably reduced.

The late Derek Cross had been through the tunnel on the footplate of an A3 Pacific and a Class 40 diesel and on both occasions he had been very pleased to see the other end of the tunnel, such is its evil, brooding, emotive reputation. The construction of the tunnel was very difficult in the Victorian age, men were killed during the excavations, and the depth of 500ft below the surface at one point exposed numerous problems.

Situated below a hill between the valleys of the Ribble and Eden the bore marked the determination of the LMS to refuse to be beaten by obstacles that could be over-come by sheer practical means.

The acrid, choking fumes eventually found their way up through the ventilators on the top of the hill and the height of steam motive power over one hundred trains per day passed through Blea Moor Tunnel. The tremendous build-up of soot on the tunnel roof tended to clog up the apertures of the brick ventilators so a 'blow back' effect was often experienced by footplate crews.

A correspondent, Mr A. W. Kewish of Barrow-in-Furness, Cumbria, tells of his experience in Blea Moor Tunnel. Mr Kewish wishes to state that neither he nor his wife are psychic.

The Kewishs were on a rail tour over several routes not usually used by passenger trains. The tour was to the Worth Valley, via Blackburn, the Settle and Carlisle, Newcastle and Keighley. What our friends did not realise was that they had to travel through Blea Moor Tunnel. They travelled up the goods line from Blackburn waited for a clear road at Hellifield Junction, got onto the long drag and worked up to the summit. The coaching stock was six or eight a side compartment type with sliding top lights, it was warm in the carriage by the time the tunnel was reached, so a top light was opened. Neither Mr nor Mrs Kewish had any idea what was in Blea Moor Tunnel but they were both very frightened, their one desire was to get off the train as quickly as possible!

They were appalled by the sickly, overpowering, cloying sweet smell that pervaded the carriage, Mr Kewish described it as not dissimilar to incense! Mrs Kewish vowed that she would never, ever travel through Blea Moor Tunnel again. There would appear to be some untold facts about Blea Moor Tunnel as there has been much speculation but very little facts of details. The bore has an evil reputation, whether deserved or not, and perhaps because of its lonely location the emotive nature of a one-and-a-half-mile hole through a hill. Perhaps one day someone in the know will explain in great detail the mysteries of Blea Moor Tunnel.

58

THE BALCOMBE TUNNEL
GHOSTS

Train spotting had hardly become an attraction for the boys of the day when the first Easter excursion thundered through Balcombe Tunnel en route to Brighton. It was no ordinary train, but one made up of fifty-seven carriages and hauled by no less than six locomotives that ran the fifty miles from London to the 'Daphne' of the Metropolis, as Brighton has sometimes been called (to quote from *The London Illustrated News* of 7 December 1884); the journey took four and a half hours.

Probably as the snorting monsters emerged from the Black Hole of Balcombe in a cloud of smoke and steam, a merry crowd of villagers who watched from the top of the embankment gave a wary cheer and wondered what the world was coming to! A hundred years on and the scene at Balcombe is much the same; trains faster and far more frequent are still thundering through the tunnel but without the cheering villagers to wave them on their way.

When England was at war and sentries were posted at both ends of the tunnel, one night, early in the war, German planes droned over and dropped bombs along the railway line possibly aiming to destroy the tunnel and so to cut a supply link to the Channel ports and the British armies in France.

Mr E. Myer of Guestling, Sussex, well remembers the night he was on sentry duty from midnight to 2am; several bombs fell close to the tunnel entrance and he decided to take refuge in one of the recesses let into the tunnel walls. After about five minutes he saw a strange sight of what he took to be three men approaching; he challenged them in the usual way and shouted, 'Halt or I fire.' At this the figures became somewhat vague and hazy and then they vanished.

As Mr Myer had been on duty under somewhat arduous conditions for several months he decided that his nerves were playing tricks on him and that he was having hallucinations.

The next day however, on his next tour of duty he met the foreman platelayer when he arrived for work. The latter commented on the air raid and that he never expected to see soldiers guarding the tunnel, especially inside the tunnel for a second time, it having been guarded during World War I. The foreman told him that three soldiers had been killed near the spot that Mr Myer had been in the recess the previous night, they had apparently been run down by a train just inside the tunnel mouth. Today the London to Brighton trains still roar through Balcombe Tunnel, the passengers completely unaware of the tragedy that will haunt the darkened bore for ever.

THE STRANGE HAPPENINGS
AT INGROW TUNNEL

There are many unexplained events on the Keighley and Worth Valley line that runs from Keighley to Oxenhope five miles further up the branch.

The strange occurrence at Ingrow Tunnel has not been explained by logical reasons and so must be regarded as, maybe, a paranormal phenomenon.

Ingrow Station is at present being rebuilt by the lively society that supports the Keighley and Worth Valley Railway Company, as part of a complete refurbishment of the unique branch.

However, the strange events at Ingrow Tunnel take the shape of black smoke billowing out of the tunnel, obviously emanating from a steam locomotive, which is very possible considering the K&WVR has plenty of steam motive power. but on the occasions that we are concerned with none of The Society's locos had been in steam so therefore cannot be blamed for the incident.

Two men, Supervisor D. Narey and his pal Arnold Illingworth, say the smell was remarkably like that of a steam engine. They have investigated the source of the smoke and although they walked the tunnel they have found no explanation except the phenomenon seemed to stop in a recess under the Halifax Road. Another strange point of the mystery is that the two men claimed that the smoke came out of the tunnel mouth towards the station yet a breeze was blowing the other way. Mr Narey ruled out smoke from nearby factories or bonfires in the Wesley Place area. Workers from VOLSEC have spent the last year renovating the Ingrow Station and plan to replace the station buildings next year so I wonder if anything unexplained will be found then?

Railway official Graham Mitchell says the original tunnel builders were plagued with problems including part of the nearby Wesley Chapel sliding away. 'We don't know that anyone was killed or injured near there so there shouldn't be anyone haunting it.'

59

THE GHOST

AT BOX HILL TUNNEL

Box Hill Tunnel is quite a long tunnel. It is in fact one and three quarter miles long, which is a lot of tunnel to maintain for any permanent way gang, whom I don't imagine relish the thought of working in the dark, damp, gloomy bore. It was built by Isambard Kingdom Brunel in 1841 and at the time it was acclaimed as an engineering masterpiece.

To many early rail travellers, however, the gloom of the tunnel was very frightening. They had some very funny ideas about the construction as it was some 300ft below the surface and some of the local people feared the whole land area would collapse. Fears were also expressed by some passengers that the tunnel might collapse while they were travelling through it or that they might suffocate from the lack of air because it was one and three quarter miles long!

However, in the latter days of steam, maintenance workers while near or inside the tunnel were absolutely convinced that they heard the sound of an approaching train. In fact some of them swore that they saw a phantom train roaring into or out of Box Hill Tunnel; of course the sceptics laughed their heads off at such a far-fetched tale but the more psychic were inclined to accept the men's story. Certainly many gangers refused to work in, or near, Box Hill Tunnel, such was the reputation it earned.

Tunnels are so emotive and the mind can conjure up thoughts of terror and the possibility of being run down in a dark tunnel. The mind runs riot at what might happen.

60

FIND THE LADY

Long train journeys are often very boring and tiresome, especially if you are on your own. The monotony is relieved somewhat if you have the opportunity to talk to a fellow traveller who feels the same about long train journeys, then you have something in common besides moaning about the rigours of train travel. Often people who share your compartment wish to relax and do not wish to indulge in polite conversation, they may just want to read a newspaper or magazine so we must respect their wishes.

However, our story concerns a couple, Mr and Mrs Wishart, who in the autumn of 1945 had occasion to visit relatives in Newcastle. The Wisharts, who lived in North London, were not looking forward to the long train journey one little bit; being just after the war, the trains were run down, lacked essential maintenance and didn't keep very good time, so the Wisharts regarded the prospects of the journey with considerable misgivings.

The Wisharts had to catch the 10.30am train from King's Cross and to their amazement they found few people in the usual queue; they had bought newspapers and magazines to read on the journey and when they found an empty compartment they settled down. The windows were fairly clean – well, you could see through them – the layer of dust on the woodwork was thinner than usual and the compartment was reasonably warm.

The train left King's Cross on time and the Wisharts began to read their newspapers, not much conversation took place as they were absorbed with their reading, an occasional smile and a feeling of companionship was enough.

An application of brakes slowed down the clickety-click of the rail joints. Mr Wishart looked out of the window, they were running through a maze of sidings packed with every kind of rolling stock, the tall chimneys of the brick works dominating the sky line, 'I think this is Peterborough dear,' he remarked. His wife consulted her watch, 'On time too, that is good!' she said. The long train eased into Peterborough Station and the train announcer called 'Peterborough'. A few people were on the platform, the station staff busied themselves with mail bags and other items of luggage and parcels, at last the guard blew his whistle. The Wisharts were about to settle down to their reading when the corridor door slid open and an elderly lady eased her way into the compartment; the newcomer was wearing a striking black silk dress and black hat which were very reminiscent of the Victorian age. The lady was carrying a wicker basket measuring 2ft by 1ft; it was white and to Mrs Wishart it was typical of the lady's attire. The lady smiled and sat down opposite the Wisharts, she carefully placed the wicker basket on the seat next to her, then folded her arms and composed herself in relaxation. The Wisharts resumed their reading, Mrs Wishart kept glancing at the old lady – she couldn't help admiring her dress, it was so Victorian and really out of place in 1945.

The motion of the train, the clickety-click of the rail joints, had a somewhat soporific effect on Mr Wishart and he found himself nodding off. No conversation took place between the three people on the part of the journey between Peterborough and Grantham. Mr Wishart slept and in fact he snored but the old lady was silent, obviously completely composed.

At last the train pulled into Grantham and Mrs Wishart nudged her husband, 'Can you get us a cup of tea, love?' she asked. And in a whisper, 'Perhaps she', looking at the old lady, 'would like one too?' Mr Wishart opened the carriage door and asked a porter how long they had to wait. Had he got time to get a cup of tea? The porter glanced at his watch 'If you hurry sir.' Mr Wishart hurried off to the refreshment room, luckily got served straight away and with difficulty got back to the compartment just as the guard was blowing his whistle; the old lady took one of the paper cups of tea and murmured her thanks.

The Wisharts read the remaining news in their papers and looked out of the window, the old lady was still silent and motionless. The Wisharts kept giving her a look but her eyes were closed and she looked very serene and still.

Eventually Durham was reached and the long train drew into the ancient city. As the brakes came on and the flurry of activity again took in more passengers and luggage the old lady stood up and moved to the door. Mr Wishart stood up and opened it for her, handing her the wicker basket which seemed surprisingly light; the old lady stepped off the train onto a now deserted platform. She turned and said, 'I wish you many happy years'. Then as Mr Wishart was about to say 'Thank you', to his surprise she vanished into thin air. Mr Wishart couldn't believe it. He stepped down onto the platform looking around but there was nowhere she could hide, as if she would! He darted about looking to satisfy his astonishment but the old lady had melted away. The guard blew his whistle, Mr Wishart climbed back into the compartment and sat down. 'Where's she gone, dear?' asked his wife. 'I can't understand it, she just vanished,' he gasped. Then he noticed the third cup with some dregs of tea remaining in it! It hadn't been a dream, or had it?

61

THE REPLAY OF
THE TAY BRIDGE DISASTER

On 28 December 1879 Sir Thomas Bouch's fine example of engineering, the Tay Railway Bridge – over which Queen Victoria had so graciously travelled, pausing on the other side to bestow a knighthood on the brilliant engineer – was overwhelmed by a violent storm, high winds causing the structure to collapse into the foaming river below. Unfortunately, an engine and five coaches were on the bridge at the time and the ninety passengers were drowned.

Local people though, still maintain that every year on the anniversary of the accident, a ghost train crosses the bridge from the Edinburgh side. Its red rear lamp trails into the darkness and finally vanishes . . . just as the Signalman saw the doomed train all those years ago.

The first Tay Bridge showed up the lack of expertise and foresight required for such a structure, no wind tunnels or sophisticated testing were available to the engineers in the late 1870s. Bouch's bridge was made mainly of wrought iron and did not allow for the movement so essential in bridges of that type.

The reappearance of the ill-fated train on the anniversary of the tragedy is not taken lightly by the local inhabitants and there are many people who will vouch for the authenticity of the phenomenon.

62

THE LITTLE OLD GUARD

A strange apparition was witnessed by a lady about two years ago on a section of track between Barking and Upminster in Essex. The lady was travelling on this particular journey which was subject to many delays owing to permanent way maintenance work, and the passengers were heartily fed up with the hassle. Several times they had to step down from the train and walk along the track to the nearest station; on this particular evening the passengers were all wanting to get home and any delay was not welcome.

Our lady who kindly offered me her account of the happenings was returning home from a hospital visit. It was around 6pm, very dark; suddenly the train began to slow down to a crawl, 'what now?' thought the passengers. Then to everyone's surprise they saw on the side of the track a little old man perhaps in his seventies, wearing an old-fashioned waistcoat and jacket, standing in a brick arch-shaped embrasure looking anxiously at the train. As we drew near he took a step forward shining his lantern with its green light above his head as if to give the driver the 'All Clear'. Our correspondent smiled to herself, no doubt thinking that the railway company must be short of staff if they had to bring such an old man out of his back garden to work the system.

Since that occasion my correspondent has tried to find the embrasure or refuge that the old man was standing in, without success. It simply isn't there, even the wall doesn't exist. The whole scene to my informant was as clear as a bell, but on reflection it would seem as if it was part of an earlier railway system. She is absolutely confident that she was privileged to witness a scene from the past in startling clarity that would continue to baffle her for ever.

63

TULSE HILL STATION

Mr Jack Hallam's excellent book *Ghosts of London* tells of the unexplained sounds of heavy footsteps heard by staff at night at Tulse Hill Station. Footsteps are heard ascending the stairs to platform 1 passing clean through the locked barrier gates and proceeding along the platform.

The footsteps are said to be those of an unfortunate platelayer who was killed shortly after the introduction of the electric trains. On the fateful night he ascended the stairs, passed through the barrier and greeted the porter on duty and then he walked down onto the track. It was a blustery, windy, cold night and knowing that a down steam-hauled train was due, he stepped onto the up line instead of the safety of the trackside cess. It is thought that the sound of the approaching steam train and the prevailing gale prevented him from being aware of the electric train's presence.

He was run down and killed, but he was so attached to his job that he still wants to keep his eye on his old work place. Today certain people will not go on the station after dark, so the past tragedy lingers on over an entire railway complex.

64

CUBBAGE FROM THE PLAIN

This is a story of a misunderstanding that reduced a man to suicide, also the love affair that fell foul of the postal system and tragic circumstances, the combined forces of fate culminating in the tragedy. The lady concerned is left completely distraught, and a restless, searching ghost that never finds peace and affection.

Mr Cubbage was an Indian, dark, and very handsome. He had settled in Ireland many years ago and through his shrewd business ability and financial acumen he had become very wealthy.

Just after World War II he bought a large mansion 'on the Plain' and restored it to its prior magnificent glory and settled down to enjoy his wealth. There was only one thing he lacked and that was a wife. Mr Cubbage must have seemed a good catch with his fine house, handsome looks and with his obvious wealth. Could any girl resist these assets?

Mr Cubbage, however, was very circumspect in his choice of lady friends and he realised that he could be the target for any gold-digging female. He looked around very carefully and finally met a young lady with whom he fell head-long in love. Their mutual affection was genuine and Mr Cubbage was overjoyed at his good fortune; he entertained his young lady, who we will call Coleen, to the best things in life. He heaped presents of jewellery, furs, motor cars, travel, expensive restaurants, days out hunting, on her; in other words Mr Cubbage was trying to sweep the young lady clean off her pretty feet.

Mr Cubbage wanted to get married without further delay. Coleen, however, although she loved Mr Cubbage, wanted time to think things over and would gently scold him for his haste. Coleen listened to his amorous overtures of love never doubting his sincerity, but she still wanted to be sure and she tried to gently tell him so; she had to be sure before she said 'yes'.

Her lover, however, was not to be put off. He wanted an answer quickly, he wasn't used to delay of any kind and kept up the pressure, 'Please give me your answer,' he implored. And he pressed his suit so forcibly yet kindly. He loved Coleen with all the breath in his body, he would do anything to please her to be his wife. Coleen was not going to be rushed and after a lot of thought she decided to go to stay with friends in England to think things over.

Mr Cubbage was like a cat on hot bricks, he was most distraught at Coleen's decision to go to England, and he bombarded her with letters and flowers; he could not wait for her return and for her to say the one word that would make her his wife.

Coleen however, was enjoying herself in England, she thought of Mr Cubbage a lot but thought she wouldn't commit herself just yet. Mr Cubbage was by this time almost demented, he had to know Coleen's decision, so he wrote an impassioned letter begging her to accept his proposal of marriage. Furthermore, he added what would be construed as an ultimatum but couched in the nicest possible terms. He wrote his plea as follows: if he hadn't had a reply from her before noon on the last day of the week (which meant return post) he would trouble her no more.

The first delivery of post came and went on that fateful day, no letter. Mr Cubbage, his heart heavy with disappointment and sadness, left his mansion and walked the short distance to the main Portadown to Lurgan railway line and awaited the passing of the next train. He walked up and down the track, waiting impatiently; he had made his mind up, he was going to lie down in front of the train. His life was meaningless without Coleen, she had not replied to his entreaties so he would end it all.

He heard the train whistle, the engine was slowing for a signal then he heard it pick up speed again. Mr Cubbage, now a broken, weeping figure lay down on the rail and waited for the train to end his life and his earthly troubles. The driver of the train didn't see him until it was too late, the engine literally cut him in half, he must have died instantly.

The next part of the story is pure circumstance but the effect might have saved poor Mr Cubbage's life.

That particular day's sailings between England and Ireland were delayed owing to bad weather so the mail was accountably held up and delays caused. It so happened that the very train that ended Mr Cubbage's life was carrying the delayed mail and in one of the mail bags was a letter from Coleen agreeing to Mr Cubbage's proposal of marriage and saying that she was coming home to her lover.

The ghost of Mr Cubbage walks the coaches of many trains searching for his beloved Coleen; he has been seen often by many people in the district, he also walks the railway tracks near the spot on which he was killed, a sobbing, totally heart-broken figure. He is said to sink onto his knee on the track and wait for the train to end his life; the train crews used to look out for the shadowy figure and shudder.

The tragedy of the whole affair becomes so pathetic as we realise that Coleen does love him and only a delay of post cost him his life.

65

THE SUICIDAL STUDENT & CO

About the turn of the century, a young medical student, who was studying at Aberdeen University, ran into financial difficulties. His father, a well-to-do fish merchant in Fraserburgh, had no idea of a student's expenses at a university like Aberdeen. Ian Watson, the student in question was a clever young man who had worked very hard to achieve his place at the higher seat of learning; he found it very difficult to manage on the pittance that his father allowed him. His father's idea of universities was narrow in the extreme and possibly based on his own education which had been one of strict discipline and the basic three Rs; he had left school at thirteen and had to work hard for very little reward. Give him credit though, he had fought his way to the top and had made good.

Ian Watson was a dedicated, somewhat highly strung young man whose intelligence would have enabled him to have passed his final exams had his father realised that a reasonable allowance was so necessary. His father obviously didn't appreciate his son's undoubted abilities. His son's request for more money met with scorn 'Come home and work with me, lad, don't mess about with them books, I need you here,' his father said.

Ian was very upset by his father's intransigent attitude but he knew what he wanted to do and that was to pursue his studies by every means possible, although by now doubts were beginning to cloud his mind.

185

Inevitably a feeling of despair enveloped him and he began to feel quite helpless; his heart was in his studies and he knew that if he could manage financially he could achieve his academic rewards, but the insufficient amounts of money his father allowed him didn't permit any freedom to relax after his studies had ended. He could see no way out and in his anguish he began to think of doing himself in; the method he would use would have to be quick and simple. After some consideration he decided that he would lie on the railway line and let a train end his life; he remembered a high bridge over the railway at Kirkston of Philorth, that would do.

He decided to throw himself off the parapet of the bridge instead of lying down on the track. He would time it just right and throw himself in front of the branch line train, he knew the train didn't go very fast but it would do . . .

In the early evening of the next day he dressed himself in his best suit and wore a clean shirt and a razor tight collar; he looked at himself in the mirror, yes, he looked good, almost handsome, one must die with dignity.

He had quite a long way to walk to the bridge, but there was plenty of time; he had taken the trouble to find out the train times and he had worked out at what time the train would arrive at the bridge – about 9pm – so he enjoyed his walk. He arrived at the bridge, walked over it then back again, he looked over the parapet at the shining metals, the line curved away round a curve; he looked around, everything was quiet, the moon had come out and there was just a touch of frost in the air. Ian climbed up onto the parapet and sat swinging his legs humming a tune; he felt quite happy now, almost cheerful, thoughts came to him, why was he thinking of suicide? He had everything to live for really, he would manage on the money his mean father allowed him. He began to sing softly, should he go through with his intention to end his life? 'That's what I'm here for,' an inner voice shouted. 'Don't be silly, why do something stupid like hurling yourself in front of a train,' the thoughts crowded his mind. He looked at his pocket watch, it showed 8.55pm, not long to go now; he was in a turmoil of doubt, what should he do? He found a cigarette, lit it and watched the smoke wreathe into the night air; he enjoyed his smoke, then climbed onto the parapet and started to walk along its broad surface. He would walk over and back then go home, life was still sweet in spite of father's mean ways. He could hear the muffled sound of the train as it plodded round the curves. Ian, happier now, ran and danced on the parapet, 'Come on train, I'm not afraid of you.' The train rumbled nearer, Ian was still jigging about on the parapet, he could see the smoke box lamp flickering, then as the train was almost on the bridge the smoke enveloped the structure as Ian was doing his Highland jig; he suddenly lost his balance and fell down onto the smoke box frame, the force of the fall did its lethal work and killed Ian Watson.

The train braked hard at the fireman's shout, 'There's a man on the line.' The few passengers on the train were thrown from their seats as Walt the driver braked hard. The driver and fireman ran up to the inert body; too late, the man was dead. His head was at a strange angle. They carried the body to the brake compartment and carried on their journey; others had jumped from that bridge and there would be more.

The unfortunate tragedy was a talking point in the district for several weeks but then slowly receded into the aeons of time. Then a reminder of the tragedy came during World War I when a Polish soldier was walking over the bridge one starlit night when he saw the wraith of a man dancing on the parapet. Then smoke obscured the bridge and a sound of escaping steam and a cry took the man out of the observer's sight. The soldier looked over the parapet and saw to his horror the vague heap of a body; he scrambled down the bank but as he approached, the vision slowly faded, there was no one there. This experience had such a dramatic effect on the Pole that he hanged himself some days later.

No further reports have been documented, but possibly

people who have seen a replay of the awful scene wish to remain silent not wishing to discuss the macabre subject. In the 1920s a local man was in a terrible state of nerves and he too visited the bridge with the one thought in his mind. Yes, he did commit suicide on that bridge but he drank from a bottle of lysol which would mean a swift but painful end. I wonder if he is seen too?

66

THE HIGH WYCOMBE FOOTSTEPS

A recent story, quite unexplained, was related to me by Mr G. Leslie who is employed by British Rail in the London area.

This story concerns the sounds of footsteps walking in the ballast; no one was seen but the sounds were very convincing and one respects the account of this mystery from Mr Leslie, who certainly didn't believe in the supernatural, preferring to find a logical explanation of this sort of thing.

However, when telling his experience to a member of the High Wycombe Station staff he found that his experience was certainly not unprecedented.

Mr Leslie had been to a railway staff party in a pub called the Flint, which is situated across the road from High Wycombe Station. Mr Leslie admits to having had a drink but he says he was by no means 'under the influence'. At about 11.20pm he left the party to catch his train back to his home at Beaconsfield.

As a northbound train had just left, the station was deserted. Mr Leslie's train was to leave platform 3 on the far left-hand side of the station which is linked by a long subway. On arriving on platform 3 somewhat early for his train, he found himself completely alone; this did not disturb him.

The night was still but a mist was descending slowly; he stood looking towards platforms 2 and 1 when he suddenly heard footsteps on the ballast approaching him. As Mr Leslie had explained earlier he was completely sober and was not given

189

to imagination, he screwed his eyes up looking for the reason for the footsteps; he couldn't see the feet but heard them quite distinctly passing him in the ballast below. At this point some other people arrived to catch the train and his attention turned to them for a split second and within that time the sound of the scrunching footsteps disappeared into the night.

Sometime later, after Christmas, Mr Leslie was on High Wycombe Station again and was talking to one of the station staff. He told him of his experience and was interested to know that the phenomenon is by no means unknown and the other went on to relate another incident involving footsteps that he heard outside the office, but when he opened the door to investigate no one was there.

On another occasion he gave chase to someone running down the platform but when he reached the platform end whoever it was or wasn't had vanished. He was certain that he was dealing with a facet of the supernatural now!

67

THE MYSTERY LIGHTS

Paranormal experiences never happen to some people. That is why they can't understand other people who are able to experience supernatural events. Research has only scratched the surface of the paranormal and supernatural phenomena, so we are left with odd cases of happenings that just materialise when least expected.

Such an occurrence happened to Mr R. J. Woodward of Ninckley and his wife and daughter when travelling home around midnight along the Watling Street (A5). They had been visiting friends, they had enjoyed their evening and the time had gone quickly so it was rather late when they set off for home.

They had negotiated the roundabout for Lutterworth and the A427 to Coventry and were proceeding north on the A5 when Mr Woodward's attention was suddenly drawn to what he first thought were three buses stood nose to tail. Before he could say anything Mrs Woodward exclaimed 'Isn't it strange to see a train at this time of night?' Mr Woodward knew the area well and there were no railways here at all; there used to be many years ago and there are still signs of the old trackbed to be seen.

Mr Woodward, being something of a railway buff, couldn't help thinking that the lights were spread out as in the old non-corridor stock, three windows to each compartment, but there was no vague outline of a locomotive, just the lights, no shape of the carriages.

The low line was closed about thirty years ago but there was never a track just where the lights were positioned; distance is deceptive especially at night, there might have been a branch line, but maybe not?

The phenomenon lasted perhaps thirty to forty-five seconds, long enough for a lasting impression to be gained but the phenomenon was very clear and distinct leaving the Woodwards very puzzled by the unexpected sight.

Mr Woodward's map of the position helps to illustrate the location of the event.

68

GHOSTS

IN A RECORDING STUDIO

The Horizon Recording Studio are housed in what is an old Victorian railway building in Warwick Road, Coventry.

A series of strange events have happened in the building which can be traced to the ghost of an old railwayman, and more recently the spirit of an art student who unfortunately got hooked on hard drugs, which combined with drink killed him after he had attended the celebration party to launch the Horizon Recording Studio. This young man died about ten years ago and the railwayman maybe thirty years before.

Mr Paul Craddock who is a director of Horizon has kindly sent me some details of the paranormal events that have earned the studio a certain reputation for experiences of the, shall we say, 'unexpected'. Certainly some famous recording artists have had some frightening moments when they have been nudged and brushed past by these two ghosts.

The young art student was about nineteen when he died; he had worked hard on the dramatic murals in the studio and then he tried mixing drugs with drink and that was fatal. The studio was once part of a railway company property and that is where the old railwayman comes in. He probably worked here and certainly his presence is very evident. The strong feeling of a presence is felt, lights go on and off, doors open and shut on their own, the shadow of a man's head is sometimes seen; but on recording sessions, many unnerving things can happen, heavy breathing down the musicians' necks, brushing past people. Footsteps are heard all over the building causing surprise and apprehension and expectancy in those visitors who have heard about the phenomena but haven't experienced it.

Strange sounds are heard live over the loud speaker monitors, some times spoiling the recordings. A famous recording artist with the group Fleetwood Mac was really frightened by one of the duo and he swears that he will never come into the building again such was his experience.

As with most supernatural occurrences one never knows just when something is going to happen and this is the case in the studio. A recording session can be spoilt completely by these two ghosts. Mr Craddock thinks that the older man is dominating the art student. The directors are probably used to the supernatural events that happen from time to time; the very fact that the building has connections with the railways has possibly something to do with the old railwayman but in what context I do not know.

69

THE NEWTY POND MOTORBIKE

This story concerns two young boys who came across the reoccurrence of a terrible death involving a young irresponsible lad who used to play 'chicken' with a motorcycle on an ungated railway crossing. This lethal game is often called 'last across', the idea being to see how close you can be to a train before it hits you or you can get out of the way.

Of course, at last a train got him and killed him in a horrible way. On one very hot night in June 1982 Dave and Tony went fishing in a rather remote area of wasteland that bordered a disused railway line. A large pond was the boys' delight and they would travel the considerable distance to the 'newty' pond, as it was nicknamed, to sit in expection for the fish to bite. The pond was situated in an area that necessitated walking though two dark, gloomy plantations that after dark were very spooky and the boys were always pleased to get through them.

However, boys will be boys and they enjoyed the fresh air and the sport of fishing, in fact the boys had been known to fish after dark at the newty pond which was very illegal! But the fishing trip that hot night was something different and it was to frighten and distress the boys.

They found their usual post at the pond and set up their gear; it was hot and very humid, they were near the gated level crossing on the old trackbed. Nothing much doing at the pond, they had set the rods up and were wandering around, looking for frogs and newts, then they returned to their rods; nothing stirred, so around 10pm they decided to call it a day. They got their rods and landing nets together and set off for home. All of a sudden theY heard the hum of a motorcycle coming towards them and they both saw a motorcycle being ridden towards the level crossing. It was travelling at high speed and the boys thought it was going to hit them, the rider was crouched over the bars obviously unaware of the boys. They threw down their fishing gear and ran as the motorcycle leapt over the embankment and crashed into the deep ditch some 15ft below. The boys heard the crash and they ran as fast as they could to get help from the police and ambulance, but when the police and ambulance got there they only found the boys' fishing tackle where they had dumped it in such haste.

The boys never went to the pond again but did hear reports from other anglers that screams and shouts came from the ditch the other side of the old trackbed, also the eerie, noisy sound of a motorcycle being ridden flat out towards the railway line.

About a year later one of the boys met an old lady who lived not far from the pond and they were discussing the strange happenings when the lady said, 'I can tell you a bit about it,' and she then proceeded to tell them about the crazy motorcyclist. 'He was mad on motorbikes and he would tear around on that wasteland near the railway, bent on killing himself, I'd say. He'd play last across with the trains, no wonder he was killed by a train, he had many near misses, he always appears on the anniversary of his death and you would see the whole incident in startling detail.'

I understand that the deep ditch that the boy and motorcycle crashed into on that fateful night is referred to as 'deadman's ditch', a horrific reminder of a foolhardy game that cost a young man his life. One of the boys, now adult, tells me that even today he shivers at the thought that is etched on his brain of being chased by a ghost on a motorcycle . . .

70

DICKY O' TUNSTEAD

The legend relating to Dicky o'Tunstead caused the London North Western Railway Company many problems and succeeded in forcing this railway company to reconsider their plans for their new line between Chapel-en-le-Frith and Buxton.

Dicky o' Tunstead is a celebrated skull who lived at Tunstead Farm in Derbyshire for some three and a half centuries. He found fame in poetry and prose, he also has the reputation of being a supernatural Robin Hood and documentary evidence of his exploits attributed to him are legion.

Suffice it to say that all attempts to evict Dicky from his rightful home have met with considerable misfortune, and disturbance of such a nature that he has quickly been restored to his home.

Tunstead Farm overlooks Coomb Reservoir between Chapel-en-le-Frith and Whaley Bridge. The LNWR's engineers had planned to take their new line across land belonging to the farm, despite objections from the owners, and this is where Dicky became involved.

It was originally intended to make an embankment across the Coomb Valley which was to be pierced by a bridge to accommodate a roadway. Soon after work began however, it was found that there were serious problems in making a secure, stable base for the embankment and thus progress was brought to a halt.

Eventually, however, the navvies and engineers overcame

the difficulties and the bridge was erected over the road and the foundations of the embankment were laid. Then before work was finally complete the arch of the bridge collapsed and the embankment at either side of the bridge was thrown up thus wrecking the whole project. A lot of time and money had been spent rebuilding the works necessary to complete the job but such were the difficulties experienced that the whole project became completely impracticable and the LNWR conceded defeat and altered the route of the line to exclude the land at Tunstead Farm.

The new work also involved the construction of a road over a quarter of a mile long but no unexpected difficulties were experienced, either with this or the realigned route of the railway.

Of course the sceptics and the doubters will sneer at the influence on the affair exercised by Dicky saying that the former route was unsuitable and geographically unstable, and they will point out that such conditions have been overcome in other parts, for example, the West Highland, the Liverpool and Manchester and the Settle and Carlisle, but then those conversant with Dicky o' Tunstead will continue to believe that it is his malign influence which kept the rails away from Tunstead Farm.

71

THE 'LUCK' OF EDENHALL

A legend concerning the London North Western Railway Company 'Whitworth' class locomotive named *The Luck of Edenhall* No 90 – what an unusual name – but then the story of how it came by the name is unusual too.

The name is derived from Eden Hall, a mansion which stands near Penrith and curiously enough within sight of the Settle and Carlisle line of the Midland Railway. Eden Hall was the family seat of the Cumbrian family of Musgrave since the days of King Henry VI; the 'Luck' is an heirloom, a beautifully enamelled and engraved glass goblet with Moorish-style decorative work on its surfaces.

How it came into the Musgrave family is as follows.

The family butler went to draw water from St Cuthbert's well in the grounds of Eden Hall one day when he came across a company of fairies dancing, and in their midst was a cup of painted glass.

The butler seized the glass where upon the fairies tried to regain the cup but realising that they were no match for this mortal they finally abandoned the struggle and vanished, leaving the butler with the glass cup and according to a ballad by the German poet Uhland with this warning.

If that glass either break or fall
Farewell to the Luck of Eden Hall

Ever since that time, the fate of the Musgrave family and

the strangely beautiful glass goblet have been regarded as inextricably entwined. The vessel is described as being about six inches tall and it has been suggested that it may have been used as a chalice, and it might have originated in Spain or Syria and been brought home to England from one of the Crusades. But whatever the origins the fairy folk warning has never been left to chance and the 'Luck' still exists; it is either locked away in a strong room on the premises or according to some accounts stored safely in the custody of the Bank of England. Eden Hall was extensively rebuilt in 1935 or thereabouts, and much of the original fabric removed at that time, today it is a girls' school.

The poet Longfellow's version of the Uhland ballad runs thus,

This Glass of Flashing Crystal Tall
Gave to my Sires, The Fountain Sprite
She wrote in it, 'If this Glass Doth Fall
Farewell Then Luck of Eden Hall'

It is from the last line of this work that the LNWR coined the name for their locomotive.

72

THE SPECTRAL TRAIN
OF KYLE!

Some supernatural manifestations are regarded as portents of good or evil; one such occurrence was the Spectral Train of Kyle. In the seventeenth century a famous visionary and seer, locally know as the Brahan Seer, predicted 'That the day will come when every stream will have its bridge, balls of fire will pass rapidly up and down the Strath of Peffery, carriages without horses will cross the country from sea to sea.' This prophecy came true when in 1870 the Dingwall & Skye Railway opened its line from Dingwall on the eastern seaboard to Strome Ferry on the west on the shores of the waters of Loch Carron.

A further twenty-seven years were to elapse before the railway reached its ultimate terminus at the Kyle of Lochalsh. However, the imminent arrival of the railway was foreshadowed by an appearance of a spectral train whose large black locomotive was seen rushing along the lonely Highland road with headlights blazing before suddenly veering off into the hills. It would seem that this apparition became a regular occurrence to such an extent that the coachman who operated a public conveyance until the opening of the railway to Kyle of Lochalsh would only run in daylight.

73

FRENCH DROVE AND
GEDNEY HILL

This station was opened by the GNR on 2 September 1867 and in 1882 the operating company became part of the GN&GE Joint Railway Company. Situated south of Postland (Crowland) on the Spalding to March line near the point where the GN line crossed the M&GN joint line at Murrow, refuge sidings were a facility at this station, to handle a considerable volume of freight traffic, mainly generated by local farmers with their produce. Passenger traffic was profitable until BR decided that this facility should be withdrawn on 11 September 1961, but the goods traffic continued until the ultimate closure of the station on 5 October 1964.

This quaintly named station was a victim of the Beeching Axe, and after closure of the station is was offered for sale as a dwelling house. The line was still open but run down and neglected, with fewer and fewer trains travelling over the weed-covered rusting tracks. After a while, general deterioration having started, a buyer was found. Mr Harold Caunt and his son moved in to restore the structure and make it into a home.

The Caunts, however, were to experience several unwanted and totally unexpected events which were to bewilder and baffle them, but let Mr Caunt explain the strange events.

'One fine day, being in need of provisions, my eldest son Terry and I cycled to the village shop in Gedney Hill. While being served by the young lady behind the counter, who had noticed that we were strangers, we were asked from whence we came. 'French Drove station,' we replied. On hearing our reply she went deathly white. 'Oh dear,' she said eventually, 'you don't want to live there, the place is haunted.'

'Now being of a practical disposition and having lived in many strange places I wasn't going to be put off by local village rumours about ghosts. We carried on the restoration work at the station; there was much to do and we were kept very busy and involved with our work.

'Subsequent events, however, were to remind us of the shop girl's warning. The mail in those days was delivered by a post lady on a bike and was usually delivered at around 8.30am. One day we were having breakfast when we heard a woman's voice from near the foot of the stairs in the hall. Expecting to find the post lady at the door Terry went to collect the mail only to find no one in view. He looked around but there was no sign of anyone. Puzzling, he returned to report, 'No one there'.

'It so happened that the post was late that day. We considered the events carefully, as we certainly did not consider ourselves as fools nor did we imagine things of this nature. We had definitely heard a woman's voice, that was certain, so we had to accept the fact that something funny was going on and we would have to see what happened in the future.

'Some time later we had a visit from a young man who worked for BR and was on holiday revisiting some of the stations that he had worked at in the past. During a conversation in which I mentioned the mystery of the woman's voice, he explained that many years ago a stationmaster at French Drove committed suicide by hanging himself from a hook in the ceiling of the room above the ticket office. His poor, distressd wife died shortly afterwards and it transpired that she used to help her husband in his duties. It became her job to close the station at night, and in the dark winter nights she used to carry a stable lantern to enable her to find her way around the dark corners of the station. Our visitor told us that her ghost had been seen by several local people at certain times of the year. So, when a lighted lamp wobbled along the track one dark, winter's night, we really cringed in terror. Luckily there was an explanation for this occurrence. We found that the husband of the crossing keeper further up the line – who worked at Perkin's engines – would ride his bike along the track when on his night shift, up on to the platform and leave it under the signal box to await his transport to work; hence the wobbly light.

'However, the mystery of the woman's voice remained a worrying event that often caused a shiver to run down our spines. Also, the stories of the sighting of the ghost of the stationmaster's wife were confirmed by the local residents, many of whom wouldn't come near the station after dark. So what now? Let us hope that the restless ghost of a distraught wife has found peace at last, certainly no logical reason has been offered to explain the strange events at French Drove and Gedney Hill station and it will continue to baffle and tantalise our enquiring minds for some time to come.'

74

THE 'UNSEEN' TRAIN

AT REDDITCH

To refer to the unmistakable sound of a train 'working hard against the grade', ethereal or paranormal, is open to debate but that is what my correspondent Mr Bernard Essex heard one early morning. As Mr Essex observes, to make up a convincing faked ghost story is difficult but to tell the incredible truth is easy because this incredible experience Mr Essex tells me is absolutely true.

Mr Essex lives in the Warwickshire village of Studley and about one mile east of the former trackbed of the railway that ran from Redditch in a generally southerly direction towards Alcester, Evesham and Ashchurch. Now all rail services south of Redditch were terminated in June 1964 and until that time Mr Essex could hear quite clearly the sound of trains from his house, most of them were steam hauled when the services ceased in June 1964. Naturally when the services ended the familiar sounds were no more, just a memory. But were they? About three months after the final operation, at about 6am one morning, Mr Essex was getting up, he was wide awake and dressing. All was still and quiet, when suddenly on the early morning breeze came the faint sound of a steam locomotive on the now closed railway line, working hard with a sharp cut off as it fought the familiar gradient. Mr Essex was utterly amazed and quickly opened the window to investigate.

The sound came louder to a final familiar crescendo then

it died away gradually to a faint whisper, then it had gone as if it had been proceeding normally on its journey.

Mr Essex assures me that the exhaust beats were clearly audible, the sounds of steam issuing from the cylinder drain cocks and the clank in the valve gear were clearly heard. the experience lasted for about three minutes.

Later that day, Mr Essex phoned Redditch Station to ask the staff about the possibility of trains running on the aforementioned line northward to Birmingham and Mr Essex told them what he had heard. Eventually he spoke to the station master who was very interested yet amused by the story. The station master explained that although the track south of Redditch was still in situ, all the points and control to single-line working and exit at the south end had been taken out and it would have been impossible for a train to leave or enter Redditch at that end.

Mr Essex of course searched for a logical explanation of this mystery; the only other operating part of British Railways in the area was and still is the Great Western line at Henley-in-Arden. This line runs about eight miles to the east of Mr Essex's home and Mr Essex assures me that it is completely inaudible, so we can discard that theory.

Even a practical joker playing back a recording of a steam train operating over that line would have to be very clever to produce a conclusive effect especially from a static position.

Mr Essex was, he believes, the only person who heard the unexplained sounds and he says although his experience cannot be corroborated he believes that there would be no point in making up such a story.

So we are left with the mysterious sounds that would seem to provide no rational explanation.

75

THE STRATEGIC RESERVE,
FACT OR FICTION?

Where did all the steam locomotives go? As the sixties drew to a close the remaining workhorses of British Railways became increasingly grimy, run down and leaked steam from every joint. The majority went to scrapyards but the lucky few were rescued by the preservation movement and although in serious states of dilapidation were restored in many cases, and now earn their keep on the increasing number of preserved lines.

However, rumours persist these days that a certain number of steam locomotives had been extensively overhauled at BR's works and stored away in remote parts of the British Isles to provide motive power in the case of an emergency. If we remember the long shed at Hartlepool's motive power depot with its two round houses where the once large fleet of engines were coaled, watered, and serviced between duties; one day they were there, next day they were gone, stored to await their fate.

In those days steam depots were depressing places and locomotives were seen in forlorn convoys being hauled away to the scrapyards. Albert Draper's yard was full of these sad, forgotten, rusting steel hulks as they waited to be broken up by the cutter's torch to be eventually recycled into razor blades or motor cars. Yet there are tales and theories to support the notion that not all the discarded steamers met such an ignoble fate. The sudden cut back in oil to British Railways and other users in 1979, which was about ten per cent, and of brief duration, fed the fabled strategic reserve rumour, especially as now the world is awash with oil!

The idea of a huge store of locomotives in a camouflaged shed or a tunnel complex beneath a mountain awaiting the call to come to Britain's rescue in a time of national crisis has all the hallmarks of King Arthur and his knights of the round table slumbering until danger threatens their kingdom. For the chivalrous sleeping heroes to be wakened by the call of a horn, imagine instead the familiar chime whistle of an A4 surging along and the emotive effect engendered in that simple act.

We will therefore look at the arguments one by one and assess their merits and real possibilities and seek the tell-tale signs that suggest contrary beliefs.

Where did all the locomotives go?

The answer to this in the majority of cases must be the scrapyards, apart from those bought for private preservation and now operating privately. Rhyd-y-mynm near Mold in North Wales is thought to be a location for a number of the strategic reserve. It is believed to be a complex of small buildings surrounded by a perimeter fence with security guards and has been noted by certain eagle-eyed people. There were ventilator shafts in the mountain to suggest underground chambers, rail connected to British Railways. Until the early seventies the track has been partially lifted but there remains a section continuing from Mold almost to its doorstep without apparent reason.

Another choice is Hessay near York, the home of the 322 Engineers Park Royal Engineers. Here tracks ran between pre-fabricated buildings with a link to British Railways' York and Harrogate line; army depots at Bicester, Oxon and Marchwood, Hampshire are other choices. The War Department has revealed that at each depot there are locomotives . . . but they are all diesels employed for the movement of stores. Marchwood speculation was boosted when it was revealed that David Shepherd's 9F *Black Prince* was overhauled in this depot albeit a high security heavily guarded complex. A comment from a letter written to the magazine *Steam Railway* was as such: 'It would be interesting to guess what equipment exists at Marchwood that could retube a 9F in 1979.' Maybe closed guarded doors, barbed wire and a lot of emotive ideas created the sort of situation of James Bond fantasies!

Which locomotives may have been retained?

The obvious choice would be those of the BR standard classes constructed under the modernisation plan, with the various types including the maximum amount of interchangeable fittings to provide maintenance economies. Built between 1951 and 1960 many 9Fs had had only nine years' service before withdrawal. Records have been kept by individuals and the RCTS through its magazine *Railway Observer* of withdrawals and dispersal points; only a handful of standards are not accounted for. There are of course a large number of locomotives of all sizes active in private hands; are these the ones that would be commandeered in the case of emergency?

Could a steam reserve still function?

The answer is certainly yes. The current number of steam excursions running on BR suggests so, removal of water troughs and columns, coaling towers and the other hardware have been successfully bypassed. Steam crews are still available, in fact BR have been training drivers and firemen to cope with the excellent business that has been generated by steam specials, coupled with the fact that BR have been busy 'thinning out' the mainline diesel classes in recent years and are always grumbling about 'lack of motive power'.

I have heard of many reports of where redundant steam locomotives may be stored. Some of the reports are highly credible, some are pure fantasy. It is not impossible for the strategic reserve to exist, remember the emotive report in the magazine *Steam Railway* – one old driver recalls an unusual tale. One Sunday, he had just come off the shed with a train of 'old scrappers' when he was stopped at a signal box. The signalman explained that he had received 'fresh instructions', the driver and fireman were to be relieved and another crew took over. The could still expect full pay, they never saw the train or whoever took it over. Here we see the mysterious interruption of journey, full pay, unexpected time off and a strange disappearance.

However, regarding the strategic reserve, there are no supporting documents, no unimpeachable testimonies, and no photographs to give the rumour credibility. Government sources have of course never divulged the location of certain important emergency measures and in the case of the hidden store of steam locomotives this blanket of security is essential. The railway enthusiast will search and try to find out whether the rumour is fact or fiction. But I hope that the mystery will be discussed at all levels, but only as a talking point, so we can only wonder and imagine a line of standard class locomotives in first class condition waiting for the chance to show the modern motive power a thing or two!

76

SECOND SIGHT?

I am indebted to Mr M. Houghton of Bolton for a very strange mystery that he was to experience during his boyhood but to this day there would appear to be no explanation. One can only think that he somehow became involved in a kind of time warp that was to bewilder him some thirty years later.

It happened when he was thirteen, and very keen on train spotting; he would, like most boys of his age, go anywhere to get engine numbers. He was an expert on the different types of engines, where they came from, where they were going to and in fact anything to do with trains the lad knew all about it. This incident took place in 1950, it was a Sunday evening in August and the location was Northenden Junction on the Cheshire lines where the main line into Stockport (Tiviot Dale) and the branch into Stockport (Edgely) diverged.

'On this particular Sunday, as on most Sundays, the signal box at Northenden Junction was switched out and the signals left clear for the main line to and from Tiviot Dale. The next box to the west (Baguley) was apparently switched out – it invariably was on a Sunday – and the distant signal was showing clear for the whole of the time that I was at the location. This left a very long section of line between Skelton Junction to the west, which in my recollection was always open and I think Heaton Mersey to the east (towards Stockport Tiviot Dale). As I was aware that excursions to and from the Lancashire coast very often passed through Northenden on a

211

Sunday, I cycled along there to see whether there would be any action, I positioned myself on a road bridge adjacent to Northenden Junction Signal Box. It was a very clear summer evening, visibility was excellent and there was full light. I waited on the bridge for about an hour, I was very patient but now began to fidget. I wanted to see some action, besides I had to be home soon as I had a paper round to do early the following morning. No one was about, I looked up and down the line, nothing in sight. I was just about to pack up and go home when I suddenly saw the smoke of a train approaching from the direction of Skelton Junction. I positioned myself on the bridge parapet, safely of course, to get a good look at the engine and the length of the train.

'When it came into view, the engine was a Stanier Class 5, or Black Five as the train spotters called them. It was hauling a train of five coaches and when it reached my position I noted the engine's number on the smoke box door as 44813. It was travelling at a leisurely pace, probably between 40 and 45 mph. I paid no more attention to it as it passed under the bridge but recorded the number in my pocket book that I always carried with me on these trips.

'I then looked up and down the line to see if anything else was in sight and noticed to my surprise another plume of smoke coming from the same direction as the other train. I quickly looked to see if I could see the last train but of course it had disappeared. I couldn't believe that two trains should follow each other so close, but it was another train all right and I was interested to see if it was another passenger working.

'Although at my tender age I did not understand the complexities of signalling something told me that all was not as it should be but by now the train was getting nearer and I was bent on taking the number of the loco.

'I remained in my position on the bridge and as the train approached I saw that it was again a Stanier Black Five hauling five carriages, same as the last one. Now for the number; again I peered at the smoke box number plate, to my surprise it read 44813. I was puzzled, the train was running again leisurely at between 40 and 45mph, same as the last one, I thought, very strange! I opened my pocket book, there on the page was the number of the previous train, 44813, I couldn't believe it. It would appear that I had been caught up in something queer at that time, the thought of a time warp did not enter my mind. Years later I did wonder about the possibility of a time warp but even then was not sure what one of these things was.

'The possibility of a mistake on my part never entered my mind, at thirteen train spotting was a very serious business and we were all eagle-eyed and mistakes did not happen.

'Over the years I thought from time to time about those mysterious happenings, the memory is still very clear in my mind and although I have been over and over it in my mind the facts remain completely unsolved.

'One thing is certain, what were two trains doing running so close together? That alone is a complete mystery.'

77

THE TRAIN IN THE NIGHT!

The village of West Dereham lies on a branch line that served four villages, Denver, Ryston, Abbey and West Dereham and the terminus at Stoke Ferry. The Great Northern line that runs south from King's Lynn to Ely and the branch line was situated almost half way between the two towns. Passenger traffic was withdrawn on 22 September, 1930 and final closure to goods and the cessation of railway services took place on 31 January 1966.

The feature of our story, West Dereham, was formerly known as Abbey, then was West Dereham on 1 January 1886. The name was changed again on 1 July 1923 to Abbey and West Dereham and that is how it stayed until the closure of the station.

Mr A. Dixon of West Bridgeford near Nottingham writes to tell me of a very strange occurrence that happened to him and his wife whilst they were living in West Dereham in 1954–5.

Mr Dixon worked on a local farm on the outskirts of the village, which in those days only had the benefit of a goods service, which I suspect only ran when demand warranted it. The farmers used it to convey their produce, and general goods were carried on occasions.

One night Mr Dixon woke with a start, he could hear a noise; he leapt out of bed and peered out of the window. The Dixons' house commanded a view over the railway where it ran through the village. Mrs Dixon, waking up, wanted to

214

know what the excitement was about. She soon joined her husband at the window; they both listened, they could hear the sound of a train coming to the village, the clear night seemed to amplify the unmistakable sound of a steam engine getting nearer. They looked at each other, then peered out of the window again, then they saw it – an engine pulling two coaches passing slowly along the rusting line. As it slowly chuffed out of sight the Dixons were puzzled, where would a passenger train be running to at around 3am, who would be opening the gates and operating the signals? Still wondering they returned to bed and sleep.

The following day Mr Dixon mentioned the incident to his workmates on the farm. They looked at each other and grinned, one man said 'You've been dreaming, no passenger train has run down this line for years.' But the Dixons were adamant, they knew what they had seen and it was very real to them and neither could be accused of romancing or being under the influence of drink.

Mr and Mrs Dixon went to have a look at the line; it was very rusty and overgrown and there was no sign of anything having travelled on it for a long time, although the goods did use it occasionally.

No solution has been offered to solve this incident and so it will remain an unanswered mystery.

78

A STRANGER IN THE FOG

This story is one that is timeless and it loses nothing for repeating. Its drama is retained and although it goes back to 1917 it could have happened many years later.

Henry Kirkup didn't believe in ghosts, he was a contented man, fond of his pint of beer and a bet on the horses, but one thing was absolutely certain, he was level-headed and had no time for ghosts. If anyone of his acquaintances admitted to having seen a spook Henry would laugh him out of the room.

However, after his experience with a ghost Henry was a changed man and no longer laughed at tales of the supernatural.

One winter's evening in 1917, Henry, a sergeant in a northern regiment, was hurrying down Westgate Road in Newcastle where he owned a trim little home. He was groping his way through a particularly thick, acrid fog which had descended like a blanket over the area. Henry was making for Newcastle Central Station and he had nearly lost his bearings when a voice came to him out of the gloom. 'Are you lost, mate?' Henry gasped in surprise. 'I want to go to Central Station,' he replied. 'That's all right,' replied the voice, 'I'm going there myself, keep close and we'll get there somehow.' Henry gratefully fell in beside the stranger who had now emerged out of the fog.

Westgate Road was very quiet, the muffled sounds from the industrial premises seemed strangely muted, the air was damp and cold, it penetrated the clothing. The fog was acrid and make talking somewhat painful so the two men didn't try to converse. As they passed through pools of light carved into the fog by the hissing gas lamps Henry Kirkup took a glance at his companion who was now revealed by his flashes to be a sergeant in a southern regiment. Henry noticed, however, that the soldier's uniform was of a kind worn in the South African War some sixteen years earlier. Henry was just going to ask the other why he was wearing such an outdated old uniform when the stranger spoke. 'Are you going back to your unit?' Henry said he was.

'So am I,' said the other, 'I have to catch a train from here to London.'

'I too,' said Henry. 'We could travel together, for company of course.'

'Sure,' replied the other, 'I'll be pleased to have someone to talk to.'

On arrival at Newcastle Central Station they found the train waiting, they soon found an empty compartment. By this time the fog was beginning to clear and Henry could see one or two stars glowing faintly in the winter sky.

'This night is similar to one night in 1899. I will never forget it,' the stranger remarked.

Henry was interested, 'A long time to remember 1899!'

'I have very good reason to remember it' said the South African sergeant. He blew his nose, 'I'll tell you about it. I was pleased with myself that night. I had found an empty compartment and I settled down to doze a little; then a man got in, and sat down opposite me looking at me in a shifty way, he looked mean, and ill at ease, but I was tired, I'd done a hard day's work recruiting for the regiment in Newcastle. I felt in my pocket for a cigarette and I accidentally pulled out my wallet and my pay packet which spilled out onto the floor. I picked it all up but the other man was watching me intently like a dog watches a rabbit. I was almost dropping off to sleep with fatigue when the man leapt up and made a lunge at me, he had a long knife. I grabbed his wrist and deflected the blade of the knife whereupon we both rolled about on the floor.'   Henry asked, 'Did you win the fight?'

'No,' said the stranger. 'Although my attacker was very thin he was stronger than me and as I tried to reach the window communicating cord he pulled me back and plunged the knife into my chest.'

'But were you lucky? Did you deflect the blade into a less vulnerable spot?' asked Henry feeling slightly sick at the gruesome description of the fight.

'No,' said the other, 'I was unlucky, he did not miss, he killed me.'

'He did what?' gasped Henry, looking across the compartment. He couldn't believe his eyes, the stranger had gone, dissolved into thin air. Henry was on his own in the compartment as the train drew further and further away from Newcastle.

79

THE VISITOR

I cannot think of a more bizarre situation than when one goes into a platelayer's hut to have a snack and sit quite comfortably munching away when a ghost walks in and goes to the far corner and stands gazing into the dark recesses. Such is the experience of my correspondent Mr C. Whitehead, who kindly sent me his memories of the startling event.

The story begins in the late 1950s when Mr Whitehead was employed by British Railways as a platelayer on the main line between Ramsbottom and Helmshore. This was before Dr Beeching wielded his axe with such malignant venom on the railways of Great Britain. The line was losing money, mainly due, I suspect, to the diversion of passenger traffic to make a case for closure.

Shortly before Mr Whitehead arrived to take his part in the maintenance of the line, two members of the gang were having a go at each other, niggling at first, but feelings were strained between these two men and matters were getting worse.

Then one day the two men were nearly at one anothers' throats and it took the others in the gang to keep them apart. One of the gang was walking the length, looking at the condition of the track, checking the fishplates, possible broken rails, and pumping ballast, when he came across a platelayers' cabin with the door open; fearing the cabin had been broken into and the tools stolen he ventured inside. He had hardly got inside the building when he was killed by a vicious blow from an axe wielded by one of the quarrelling men who had killed the wrong man! From then on the cabin was known as 'The Murder Cabin'.

It was some time later when Mr Whitehead came across the spectre of the murdered man who had made his presence known to several permanent way workers; they had nicknamed him 'George'.

Mr Whitehead was walking his length, the weather had been threatening rain and when the heavens opened, Mr Whitehead had to run for cover. Seeing the cabin nearby he raced to it and sought shelter; it was dark in the small building but it was dry and it served a purpose. He hadn't been there long when a shadow fell across the door, a man walked in and went over to the far corner and stood silently. Mr Whitehead shivered, it had suddenly turned quite cold. The rain was still coming down fast, the stranger didn't move, and Mr Whitehead didn't seem very menaced by the other presence so he sat still and waited for the rain to stop.

Eventually the rain stopped and the sun came out, Mr Whitehead got up and walked out into the fresh air. The stranger followed him and disappeared into the air like a puff of smoke, our friend couldn't believe his eyes. Some weeks later the whole gang were crushed into one of these cabins to shelter from the elements. The air was thick with smoke and the earthy smell of human beings crushed together. The door opened and 'George' walked in, he glided through the men to the far corner and stood in his usual posture gazing into the darkness. Mr Whitehead then told the foreman of his experience of meeting George in the old cabin. The foreman didn't laugh or pour scorn on Mr Whitehead's revelation, he just said, 'Don't worry, he won't hurt you, he often comes in to see us.'

I understand his murderer was caught and paid the ultimate penalty for this dreadful crime.

Today the track and other infrastructure has been removed

between Ramsbottom and Helmshore and so too have the old platelayers' cabins. I wonder if 'George' still wanders about looking for the cabins that he used to frequent in search of his old workmates . . .

80

GHOSTS AT KIDLINGTON

On Christmas Eve 1874, a train packed with people returning home for the seasonal festivities was derailed when an axle broke on one of the carriages near Shipton-on-Cherwell. Eight carriages left the track and plunged down a steep embankment between the bridges over the River Cherwell. Thirty-four people died in the resultant fire and crash, and over a hundred were injured.

Now a remarkable series of events have happened in a modern terraced house at the Moor, Kidlington, less than a mile from the scene of the tragedy. Ask Mr Brian Beck if he believes in ghosts. Mr Beck lives at the Moor which is the terraced house I have mentioned – and Mr Beck will answer 'I haven't any choice, have I?'. It isn't imagination when you're lying in bed and you suddenly see the figure of a child move across the room and disappear through a closed door.'

Many other things happen too in the Beck household; babies are heard crying, a poltergeist is very active moving things all over, lights go on and off, doors open and shut on their own, sounds of footsteps are heard all over the house.

At a Tupperware Party held in the house, several ladies were astonished when scratching and tapping noises were heard to come from a glass-topped coffee table. One lady had to be taken home in a very distressed state swearing that she would never enter the house again.

Mr Beck has been visited by the ghost of a lady who

materialises in solid form, no haze no mist but absolutely life-like. Her visits are nocturnal and she arrives through the closed door and approaches the bed; on one occasion Mr Beck awoke to find this lady, dressed in black and with a very sorrowful face, peering at him. Again when Mr Beck was reading in bed one night the lady appeared and put the light out. Mr Beck describes her as under forty, dressed in black, her hair done up in a bun, or tied neatly back under her bonnet; she seemed to be around for possibly thirty seconds to one minute. Mr Beck didn't feel very scared, more curious to find out her identity; she disappeared as mysteriously as she arrived.

Mrs Beck described an incident concerning her son Kye, only two and a half years old at the time, and certainly not able to use a pen. He surprised his parents by drawing a star of David in a neat and steady hand. He often said to his mother, 'I can't get to sleep, please tell the children to leave the toys alone.'

A neighbour has gone on record as seeing a woman and two children, followed by a man, walking towards the house, up the garden path then just disappearing . . . 'Cold' spots are noted in the house; one peculiar event was the morning Mrs Beck came down to find the gas cooker 'sparkling clean'; one spot near the bathroom has a strong smell of ripe apples, other smells in the house are of burning ashes and cooking, but not of this world!

How do we relate this bizarre litany of events with the horror of the train crash?

Some of the victims of the accident were taken to Hampton Gay Paper Mill to await identification; an artist from *The London Illustrated News*, in an issue dated January 1875, described the appalling scene.

One instance, I witnessed, of heart-rending grief will remain indelibly imposed on my mind. Among the dead lay a young and handsome youth of about twenty-one awaiting identification. Hearing the rustle of a lady's dress close by my attention was fixed on the lady who had just entered. She was anxiously scanning the many bodies and in a moment singled out the handsome features of the dead boy. She fell prostrate with grief over the cold, white face of her son, raining kisses on his lips that could never return her love. Beside

223

her was the father sobbing uncontrollably, silently watched by a policeman.

How does the drawing of the woman made by the artist shortly after the accident compare with Mr Beck's nocturnal visitor? Mr Beck says there is a striking resemblance and the expression on her face is always the same; but why does she always come to this house when the crash happened nearly a mile away all those years ago?

With the coaches catching fire as of course they would, as they were wooden and were lit by gas, that would account for the strong smell of burning ashes experienced by the Becks. Mr and Mrs Beck have, however, decided to continue to live with the phenomena and do not intend to move.

A family who lived in the Beck's house previously also heard strange noises and heavy distinct footsteps in a bedroom. They didn't stay . . .

It would seem that the paranormal events are tied in closely with the train crash and the lady in black is still looking for her son. Is it possible that some of the victims might have been taken to a building on the site of Mr Beck's house?

One must admire the courage and resilience of the Becks who will not allow a supernatural force to drive them out of their house.

81

GAS LAMPS AND GHOSTS?

It was a dark night in November 1981, I was the crossing keeper at Damens Station and was waiting for the passage of the last down train from Keighley. The station stood empty, a light covering of frost lay illuminated by the incandescent glow from the gas lamps on the platform. Inside the signal box, the gas lights were also lit and the fire in the pot-bellied stove was glowing red hot.

I looked across at the empty station house, there was no one stopping there tonight. It was often empty now, Annie had left after her husband Norman died last Christmas; the nearest life was the main Halifax road about half a mile up the hill, what a lonely outpost!

At least I had already brought in the lamp from the up home signal. I had just to see the last train up the hill, then lock the gates, bring in the gate lamps and the down home lamp, lock up the signal box then go home.

Where was the train? It should have left Keighley five minutes ago. The clock ticked away, ever so slowly, it seemed. From my couch I glanced up the line towards the loop, I couldn't see the loop box from the cutting, just the rods of the loop's down starter signals, and my own reflection in the glass, but what was the shadow behind me looking into the box? I froze; at least the door was bolted, the shadowy figure moved off down the platform, or so it seemed from the reflection. I pulled myself together and dashed out of the door . . .

225

'Who's there?' expecting to hear one of the local gypsy lads running off. But not a sound. A shiver shot down my back, I lit a cigarette and went back into the box, bolted the door and sat down again, where was that train?

I looked up the line again, all I saw was my reflection, and then that shadowy figure again, it was clearer this time and appeared to be wearing some sort of railway uniform. It certainly had a peaked cap but no visible face!

I spun round and dashed outside straight away; not a sound, no one was there, just an uncanny silence. The river was silent as was the little stream at the end of the platform, even the normally busy main road was quiet now. What was that? A loud shriek told me that the Midland 4F had whistled for the foot crossing, the train was here at last. The staff at Keighley must have been eager to get home as they hadn't phoned. I darted to the crossing and opened the gates, getting the down home signal pulled off just in time. The train stormed through the tiny station unaware of the goings on there, I belled the train on to the next station. I closed the crossing gates and was up and down the signal like a cat after a bird. I pulled the shutters down, turned the gas off, locked the door and dashed off home.

I mused, were the gas lamps playing tricks? Or one of the gypsies, or was it really a ghost? What ever it was I have taken steps to make sure that I have not been there alone at night from that day to this!

82

THE MAN IN THE MIST

If one is to believe statistics, only two per cent of the world's population are gifted with 'second sight' or the ability to witness paranormal phenomena, but how many of these fortunate or unfortunate people ever realise this power? It will happen to them maybe once in a lifetime, often with horrific memories of their experiences. The following story is an example of an incident that left an indelible mark in my correspondent's memory.

Mr Alistair Robertson was returning to his home in Edinburgh after a business trip to London. On arriving at King's Cross he found a seat in the 'open plan' coach, put his case on the luggage rack and settled himself down for a good read. The coach was quite full with the usual business executives chatting away. Alistair had made the journey many times and thought he knew every mile of the journey intimately. He had bought a paperback at the W. H. Smith bookstall at King's Cross; it was a war story and certainly nothing to do with the supernatural so after reading the daily paper he started to read his new book. At this stage I must inform the reader that Alistair Robertson did not tell anyone of his horrific experience for many years, the incident being so incredible and beyond belief.

The coach he was in was alive with the usual hum of conversation and noise, not offensive but somewhat soporific and he began to nod off. He felt himself falling asleep and shook himself to shake the fatigue out of his system, he opened the ventilator and the breeze was most refreshing. The clickety-click of the rail joints seemed louder and made a reassuring sound and after a while he closed the ventilator and read some more of his book.

After about one and a half hours the train entered a tunnel and it turned out to be a very long tunnel; but the story had only just begun . . . Alistair was reading his book and was somewhat annoyed when the usual carriage lights didn't come on, so he put his book down and waited for daylight to return.

But then a very strange occurrence happened, he was suddenly aware of what appeared to be a form of mist forming over the seat opposite him, this puzzled Alistair as it was absolutely pitch black in the carriage. He thought at first that it must be steam drifting in from the steam heating system but he lifted his hand to his face to find he couldn't see it. He looked at the mist again and it began to swirl about but still over the table in front of him and the seat opposite.

Alistair was becoming mesmerised by the strange experience; the mist was gradually resolving itself into the shape of an oldish man, nearly bald but well dressed in a well-cut city suit, the picture was somewhat redolent of a bank manager or some other business executive, definitely respectable. He was a happy man seemingly because he was smiling; by his face he was about fifty-five years old, fairly plump, but everything about him seemed absolutely normal. It was just the way he had appeared that was so dramatic, he had a fuzz around him that remained to tantalise and Alistair wanted to be reassured of his normality.

This mist continued to swirl about him, mesmerising Alistair who was wide eyed with surprise.

The man just sat and smiled at Alistair who was covered in confusion. Alistair noticed that amid the swirling mist behind the newcomer there appeared to be a window and through it he could see a kind of crowd of people all milling about. They appeared to be moaning and wailing as if in great distress.

The man still smiled at Alistair, putting his hands on

the table that separated them and leaning towards him. The fixed smile now became rather sinister, and began to assume grotesque proportions, he seemed to be rising out of the seat coming closer and closer to Alistair, who was now terrified and was trying to force himself back into his seat. The man's leering face was moving closer to the other face, there seemed nothing to stop it, this nightmare . . .

Alistair then thought about the other people in the carriage who were so close but so far away; the puzzling thing was that he couldn't see them or even hear them and this discovery didn't exactly help his sinking courage. As the man grew closer, Alistair could even feel the man's breath or thought he could.

Summoning up the remains of his courage Alistair thrust his hand outwards at the face to ward it off, but to his surprise he never touched anything, the man leaned back and continued to smile but again the 'smile' had become a sinister leer, menacing . . .

Then to Alistair's relief the mist's swirl was gradually dissipating, reducing the man's shape to a vague outline. Alistair shook himself, bewildered by the whole sequence of events Eventually the mist cleared completely and the man and the crowd of people behind him disappeared, the sounds of conversation of his fellow travellers returned, the sound of the rail joints were there, normality was supreme.

Alistair stood up and stretched, yawned, and looked out of the window, the passing countryside seemed so reassuring. He puzzled and gazed at the empty seat opposite, there was nothing to be seen at all. The two men sitting across the gangway were chatting happily, all seemed normal, but who was the man? And why did he appear? These questions are still unanswered and perhaps always will be . . .

83

THE MAN

IN THE BLACK BERET

This story concerns a young man who, one cold December afternoon, was incredibly caught up in a time warp that baffles him to this day. He witnessed a replay of an accident in which a man was run over by a steam locomotive. Our young man was both horrified and helpless as he saw in graphic detail this appalling accident.

Our tale begins in a very innocuous way. Young Andy had just left school and at the time of the incident, set in the 1960s, he was able to find a job with British Railways as an apprentice signalman. However, his first duties saw him very actively engaged in the removal of redundant signalling equipment, eg signals, signal boxes, etc, as part of the updating and modernisation of post-war British Railways.

Andy was working with two mates, Alf and Ron, who were older and much more experienced in the world of signalling expertise; these two men were to instruct Andy in the initial part of his training. This particular day was quite bright for December and the three men enjoyed the ten-mile journey to the local village where they had to dismantle the redundant signal cabin. The senior man, Alf, detailed Andy to remove the levers from the frame and load them into the BR van.

About 3pm Alf asked Andy if he would walk to the nearby village and get them some cigarettes and chocolate as the men wanted a break.

Andy set off for the village along the deserted track which was by now rusting. One could see the rusted track through the over-powering spread of weeds and other undergrowth. He reached the village, purchased the cigarettes and chocolate, looked round the village then started to walk back munching a bar of chocolate. He reached the old railway line and continued on his way back, this time walking on the sleepers. It was beginning to get dusk and the clouds were hastening the end of a winter's day.

He was about halfway back when he heard a noise that made his hair stand on end, the noise of a steam engine – was it possible? He looked around, nothing in sight, then faintly on the slight breeze he heard it again, the unmistakable sound of a steam engine and it was approaching. Andy knew that steam motive power had ceased in this area many years ago; anyway the line had been closed to all traffic for months so what was such an engine doing on the line now? He quickened his pace, he knew something was wrong and now felt as if he wanted to get as far away from the place as possible. Panic set in when the sound of the engine appeared much louder, he stumbled on the sleepers and fell face down. He could hear the loco as if it was almost upon him, he turned to look and an amazing sequence of events evolved before his eyes. The whole area was a haze of yellow light that seemed somehow menacing, he tried to get to his feet but for some reason couldn't, then he heard the blood-curdling sound of the shriek of an engine's whistle! It split the December air with its piercing note.

Then Andy saw the tall figure of a man dressed in railway uniform and wearing a black beret instead of the regulation railway hat; Andy thought the beret was like those worn by the Royal Tank Corps. The figure stood in the track seemingly rooted to the spot and made no move to avoid the oncoming engine. There was a horrible piercing scream from the figure as the engine struck it and ground it into pulp under the engine.

At last Andy found his feet and ran as fast as he could back to the other men; he leapt through the door and collapsed in a heap on the floor.

When Alf had revived him with a cup of strong tea he poured out his story. 'Don't be daft,' they scoffed. 'I tell you I saw him killed,' gasped Andy, 'and he was wearing a black beret like the Tank Corps wear.' Alf stroked his chin, 'A black beret'. Then the recollections came flooding back to the two older men and Alf then told Andy the story. 'I remember now, about nine or ten years ago there was a bloke killed doing track maintenance work around here, he wore a black beret and was well known. I think he had been in the Tank Corps or something like that, but you wouldn't know anything about that would you?' Andy replied that it was a bit before his time and they all laughed.

Without further ado the three men loaded the van and drove back to Darlington and vowed never to return to the area again; another gang finished the job. No further sign was seen of the phantom engine or if it was ever seen again nobody ever admitted it.

Andy is now happily married with two fine children and when they ask about ghosts Andy shakes his head.

84

THE REVENGE

OF THE OLD SOLDIER

The type of supernatural phenomenon that returns to wreak revenge for an earthly feud is fortunately in the minority, but ghosts that kill are still evident in certain circumstances.

Tom Howe was an engine driver, he was also a highly skilled engineer and in his youth had been apprenticed to a firm of railway engineers at Doncaster. He was a burly, well-built man, liked by his workmates, he had a practical disposition and he certainly didn't believe in ghosts or the occult.

In 1901 Tom moved from the North to London and he set up a family home for his wife and daughter near King's Cross Station. Later that year he met an old friend, Len Curtis, with whom he had worked at Doncaster. Curtis had moved to London earlier so it was a happy reunion when their acquaintance was renewed. Eventually Howe became fireman to Curtis on the midnight expresses to the northern capital.

When World War I began the two men served together in the 42nd Division at Gallipoli. Later, again they were to work together in the same link. Len Curtis married and Howe was his best man at the nuptials. Unknown to both men this is just where the trouble that was to end their friendship began – it would appear that the two families became very friendly and visited each others' homes regularly. However, Howe became very fond of Ellen Curtis and was taken with her charm and companionship especially as Ellen was fifteen years younger than her husband.

Tom Howe eventually became a driver and often his route would take him past the Curtis home at Finsbury Park; whenever Howe had any spare time he would visit Ellen, telling his own wife that he had business elsewhere. Eventually Ellen Curtis had a baby and the local rumours at Finsbury Park whispered that Howe was the father.

Then news of Howe's interest in his wife reached Len Curtis who was beside himself with fury; when he met Howe again he pulled Howe out of the cab of a loco and threatened him not to see his wife again.

The next day Howe was transferred to the early morning express to Newcastle via York; even so the train was on the same line that ran past the Curtis home and unknown to her husband Ellen used to wave to Howe as he passed on his regular run and on the homeward run she would wave an oil lamp.

One wet Saturday night Howe noticed from the cab of his Atlantic that Ellen's signal lamp was for the first time missing; he slowed down for the network of points near the Curtis home and whistled up but there was no sign of Ellen. As he cycled home from the shed he noticed the newsbill of the local paper, 'TRAGEDY IN RAILWAY COTTAGE, ENGINE DRIVER KILLS HIS WIFE AND CHILD THEN COMMITS SUICIDE.'

The following day Tom Howe found out that his former workmate and friend had murdered his family and then killed himself.

Time passed by with its usual routine. Howe always looked out of the cab when he reduced speed for the points and glanced at the old cottage where the Curtis family had lived, more out of habit than morbid curiosity. One night a horrific series of events occurred that was to cost Howe his life.

Tom Howe as usual moved the regulator to slow down for the points near the Curtis abode; he leaned out of the cab as usual to look for the cottage when his fireman yelled at him with a terrified look on his face. The fireman pointed to the regulator that was moving on its own into the open position. The train was now gathering speed approaching the points and Howe to his horror saw the wraith of Curtis holding the regulator wide open, but the strange thing was that Curtis was wearing the uniform of the 42nd Division, the one he had worn at Gallipoli!

Howe made a grab for the regulator to pull it back to reduce speed, but the lever was solid, no movement. Howe saw the ghostly figure disappear into the steam, the engine, by now completely out of control, hit the points at this crazy speed, derailed and hit the embankment wall. Howe was killed instantly but the fireman survived to vow that the ghost of Len Curtis had returned to wreak a terrible revenge.

85

THE VICTORIAN
RAILWAY DISASTER

Nineteen-year-old Pamela Goodsell's eyes nearly left their sockets when she saw what the light of a match revealed.

An old train, with the remains of passengers, now skeletal, lying in some disarray on the mouldering floor of the carriage. The train had been sealed up in an underground tunnel, but why?

Other remains of humans were lying all over the train; the unfortunate passengers were noticed to be wearing Victorian-style clothing, some of the men sported top hats. The teenager had fallen down a 20ft shaft while walking through the park near the site of the old Crystal Palace in south-east London.

Pamela was horrified by her discovery, yet of course very puzzled that the local authorities hadn't exhumed the remains and thus brought to light the fact of the mystery. Yet mystery there was because when she made enquiries about her find no one wanted to know. 'Completely preposterous', said London Transport. And they went on to say, 'There is no record of a subway train crash in the area.' However, that statement is certainly open to question.

The London Transport spokesman went on to say, 'We just don't lose trains and passengers like that, not even in Victorian times.'

Miss Goodsell, who said she had found the remains in 1978, could not find the shaft, however, when she went back to the park. But she remains quite unshakeable in her account of the horrific experience, and it seems that nearly all Sydenham knows that there is an abandoned underground train under the park somewhere, possibly the result of an experiment that went badly wrong, so it would appear that the story isn't all moonshine!

Legend has it that the train was shunted into a tunnel around 1870 and it was never seen again, or perhaps it was conveniently forgotten by the authorities who got the experiment badly wrong, preferring to bury their mistake for ever. One excuse put forward is that the relevant documents appertaining to the mystery were lost during the last war.

However, experts have been successful in tracing the mystery back to an experimental train designed by an engineer named T. W. Rammell, which once ran for 600 yards on a line between Sydenham Gate and Penge. Compressed air was pumped into the tunnel which had airtight doors and the train careered along at about 35mph . . . No record of any accident had been recorded, the experiment was soon discarded and no other prototype constructed; the train was evidently sealed up in its tunnel and forgotten by the outside world.

Now members of the London Underground Railway Society, I'm told, are showing a healthy interest, and I understand that they feel that they are near a break-through to crack this mystery once and for all.

The Norwood Historical Society also are interested and have combined with the former society to effect a solution. Then two societies have obtained permission to sink boreholes in the park to identify the site of the tunnel, special electronic tests have been made and are now being evaluated.

The chairman of the Norwood Historical Society has gone on record as saying that they are about to use more sophisticated electronic equipment and dig along the line of the old underground track.

The searchers are hoping to uncover the whole train intact and the outside world will be very interested to see what finds are evident. The people around the area cannot explain the occasional rumblings that are sometimes heard at different times of the year. Are they connected with this dreadful accident? Can they be explained?

86

THE WRECK

OF THE SCOTTISH MAIL

When driver Ben Fleetwood and fireman Jack Talbot reported for duty at two o'clock on the afternoon of 19 September 1906, they each had exactly nine hours left to live.

The manner of their dying was to leave behind what is probably the greatest unsolved mystery in British railway history.

Together they made a good, well-experienced, cheerful footplate crew. Fleetwood was a dignified, trusted, well-liked man of flawless character. Talbot was more than a fully competent, well-trained main line fireman. He was also a qualified driver and design engineer, and had been destined to be employed on the staff of the chief mechanical engineer.

If you were a passenger on a high-speed night express, here surely was a crew in which you could put your trust.

Their tour of duty for each day of this particular week was a straightforward little job of three separate trips.

After booking on at Doncaster sheds, they worked the three o'clock afternoon passenger train to York. From York they worked the 6.50 express to Peterborough, and from Peterborough they worked the London–Edinburgh night mail as far as Doncaster, where they were relieved and booked off duty.

This was a rostered job in the express passenger link and therefore came round to each footplate crew regularly every few weeks. Certainly Fleetwood and Talbot had worked this particular duty many times.

The engine was of a well-proven class and was virtually brand new – Jack Talbot, as part of his engineering apprenticeship, had helped to built it.

Both men knew the route thoroughly, the locomotive was hauling a train well within its capabilities, the night was dry and fine, visibility was excellent, the train was running exactly to time and under clear green signals – yet this footplate crew and twelve of their unsuspecting passengers were about to die.

At a few minutes before eleven, the train was approaching Grantham, the only stop before Doncaster.

On the platform at Grantham stood a station inspector and a small group of post office employees. They were preparing for quick action, for they had a bare two minutes in which to haul almost a hundred mail bags into the mail vans of the train once it had stopped.

On this night it did not stop. The two signalmen and the small group on the platform looked on in petrified disbelief and horror as the night mail thundered headlong into the station.

Wreathed in steam, and bathed in the crimson glow from the open firebox, the locomotive lurched along the platform in a volcanic nightmare of sound and fury. It passed safely through the station, disappeared out into the darkness at the north end of the station – then left the rails.

It was a crash of appalling destruction, a holocaust of mangled timber and metal which soon became a funeral pyre. The crackle of the flames, the hiss of escaping steam, the shouts of arriving rescuers, the screams of the dying, became a horrifying amalgam of tragic sound that stunned the senses of those further people running up to help.

The locomotive was completely and utterly wrecked. Daylight revealed it as a mangled, tangled heap of twisted steel which could give no clue to the cause of the disaster. Neither could Fleetwood or Talbot. They had been killed instantly.

The investigation – for all the light it threw on the matter – might as well never have been held.

This was no fault of the investigators. There was literally nothing to investigate, no objects to examine, no person to question and no papers to read.

The night mail had stormed at high speed through Grantham Station, raced out into the darkness – and crashed.

The stark simplicity of that statement says all that can really be said about this mystery. Various people offered a miscellany of improbable solutions, but no one explanation held much more water than any other.

If there was a popular theory, it was simply that both men had forgotten where they were on the railway line in relation to Peterborough and Grantham. But Grantham was a busy, well lit station and the two signal gantries guarding it from the south had a signal layout which was totally unique to Grantham. Either man on the footplate could read this signal layout as easily as telling the time by the town hall clock.

It was easily proved that they were both awake. The signalmen had a clear view of the footplate and both enginemen were standing on their respective sides of the footplate, the driver at the controls and the fireman standing close to the boiler front, as the train came storming into Grantham Station.

So the wreck of the Scottish mail passed into railway legend and whatever happened on the footplate of the locomotive that tragic, horrifying night – none of us shall ever know.

87

THE HEXTHORPE GHOST

My story takes place one dark night in late autumn at the Cherry Tree sidings at Hexthorpe one mile west of Doncaster. The sidings were in those days used mainly for coal and coal empties traffic, and it was while shunting empty coal wagons that the following incident took place.

My second man and myself were looking through the rear windows of our diesel locomotive awaiting a signal from the yard staff. After a minute or so the shunter signalled us with his lamp to proceed down the yard to attach a rake of wagons. As I turned to open the power controller on the loco I noticed the figure of a man coming across the adjoining tracks towards us. He appeared to be dressed in a light coloured mackintosh and cap. I lowered the cab window and shouted, 'Hey, where do you think you're going?.' He ignored my question and by now had reached the line on which we stood. Although I could clearly see his outline and had no doubt whatsoever that it was a man, I could not see his face or features, only his cap and a dark mask where his face would normally be. By now he had passed out of my sight at the rear of the loco. Turning to my second man I said, 'Has that bloke come out clear on your side?' 'No there's no one here,' he replied. At the same time we both climbed down the steps at either side of the loco and met at the rear centre. The man was nowhere to be seen. By now the shunter had walked up the siding to where we stood and asked what was wrong. I told him what had happened, the three of us again searched all around the loco and surrounding sidings, but to no avail. There was no sign of anyone. The shunter said that he had heard of the ghost of a man sitting on the buffer stops at the end of the sidings but thought that his mates were trying to frighten him. Now he wasn't so sure.

Two weeks later I was in the signal box at St James Junction which is at the opposite end of Hexthorpe yard to where the above sighting took place. I was waiting to conduct a Tinsley train crew into the Decoy marshalling yard at Doncaster. During my conversation with the signalman I mentioned the ghost. He was very startled and uneasy for a minute or so and then went on to tell me of what had happened the last time he had been on nights in that box.

He had a train of wagons bound for Wath-on-Dearne, stood in his section and the brake van was about twenty yards beyond the signal box. All was quiet when all of a sudden he heard someone shouting. Before he could get to the door of the box it burst open and in staggered a guard. According to the signalman the poor fellow was in such a state that he could neither stand nor speak. 'I sat him down and quickly made him a cup of tea,' said the signalman. After a while the guard who was in charge of the train outside the signal box was able to tell what had happened. He had been sitting quietly in his brake van waiting for the train to move off when the rear door of the van opened and a man in a light rain coat had walked in and without saying a word had gone out of the other door without opening it. In other words he had walked through a closed door. It is obvious that this was the same ghost as the one I had seen two weeks earlier. Who he was or why he was there I don't know to this day, but I do know that he *was* there and maybe still is.

88

THE LETTER

'Goodbye son,' said Mrs Ayscough, who tried hard not to weep but yielded to nature and brushed the tear away with her glove. 'Goodbye mother . . . and don't worry. We shall all be home by Christmas. They've got the Kaiser on the run already. I doubt if they'll even need us.'

But his last words were drowned in a hiss of escaping steam and Mrs Ayscough waved and waved until not only the train had vanished from view but until everyone had left the platform.

'There, there, Mrs Ayscough . . .' It was Tom Farrow the station master. 'Don't take on so. Your Bob'll be home before you know where you are.'

He put his arm gently round her shoulder and guided her to the station entrance. She went reluctantly and he watched her set off for her house down Station Road.

That night Mrs Ayscough said her prayers. She always said her prayers but that night she said her prayers more fervently than usual. She tried to imagine Bob far away in France, translating him in her mind to a foreign field. But the field she conjured up bore a marked resemblance to the field next door to her house where Bob had played in his childhood.

She thought about her son every day, prayed for him every evening and looked forward to the first letter he had promised to write to her.

But when the letter came it was not brought by the postman.

Mr Farrow the station master brought it. It was a small letter, a letter in a brown envelope, an envelope without a stamp and with OHMS written upon it.

Mr Farrow stayed with her until she had read the letter's brief sentence and he stayed with her until the light faded and until she went to bed, alone, to pray and to merciful sleep.

The following day Mrs Ayscough walked down the road to the railway station. She thanked Mr Farrow for his kindness and stood on the platform, gazing down the line, listening to the wind in the telegraph wires, looking at the silver ribbons of rail as they converged and curved away into the cutting beyond the village.

She came again the next day and Mr Farrow watched from his office window as Mrs Ayscough stood alone, keeping a solitary vigil, staring into the distance.

She did it every day. And when, in November 1918, the war came to an end, she still did it. She walked to the station in all weathers, always alone, always at the same time and stood for about five minutes transfixed.

In 1958 at the age of eighty Mrs Ayscough died. Two years later the village railway line was closed.

For some time the railway station stood empty and deserted. The signals and the signboards were all removed and, one day, the premises were bought and converted into a house.

Maureen and John Parker made an excellent job of the alterations and lived happily at Station House for many years.

As newcomers they knew nothing of either Mr Farrow or of Mrs Ayscough or of Mrs Ayscough's only son . . . until one night after Christmas in 1981.

It had been a bitterly cold day and that night a blizzard sprang up. The Parkers, snug indoors, were about to go to bed when, simultaneously they both felt they heard shouting outside.

The noise of the storm was by this time so great that both doubted their own ears. But someone seemed to be calling 'Bob' and another voice seemed to reply 'Mother'.

They stood still in the hall at the foot of the stairs, listening, craning, and John Parker stepped to the window and drew back the curtains.

Looking out across the platform he thought he could discern the figure of an old lady, standing by the platform edge staring up what had been the railway track.

And when he looked again there was another figure moving towards her, a man, a soldier . . . in a peaked cap and carrying a slung rifle.

Parker motioned his wife to join him but when he looked back there was no one there. There was no woman, no soldier, only drifting snow, driving and piling up outside the door.

Despite his wife's protests that he was on a fool's errand Parker struggled into his coat and boots and strode out into the blizzard and along the edge of the platform.

There was not a soul in sight nor were there voices nor footprints in the snow nor any living mortal thing.

He returned to the house, closed the door behind him, took off his coat shedding snow on the carpet. It was only when he took off his boots that he noticed the piece of brown paper sticking to the sole.

Carefully he removed it and, brushing the snow from it, saw that it was an envelope, a small brown envelope, an envelope with the initials OHMS stamped upon it.

And there was a letter in it, a letter just one line long, a line that began: 'Dear Mrs Ayscough, I regret to inform you . . .'

89

THE STRANGE HAPPENINGS
AT SHARPTHORNE TUNNEL

The mysteries of the paranormal will always be complex and will assume many different types of phenomena.

I have visited many disused railway stations and have walked miles of former trackbed without experiencing any feelings other than sadness and inveterate loss of a form of travel. So far I have yet to experience a ghostly sound or sighting but perhaps I am unlucky! Sometimes I wish that I could have the sense of being able to lift the veil like so many of my kind correspondents, but they tell me that I am lucky.

To some people, the ability to participate in a paranormal event seems so easy it appears as if these people generate and possibly energise the sequence of events that result in a phenomenon. Take the story of a friend of mine; a level-headed, no-nonsense disbeliever who had a traumatic experience in a disused tunnel in the south of England.

During the early 1960s, my friend was spending some time around the Bluebell Line in rural, leafy Sussex when he decided to go and have a look at the sad removal of track and facilities at West Hoathly. This station is situated north-west of Horsted Keynes which is the northern terminal of the Bluebell Line; and Sharpthorne Tunnel is situated on the line from Lewes to East Grinstead. It was a Saturday and the workmen were having their weekend off, so the place was deserted. The old station was a sad sight without any commuters to give it life. It stood empty, abandoned, left to rot until some unfeeling demolition firm would raze it to the ground; removing a way of life.

Everything was quiet and the autumn leaves were covering the ground; the now lifeless trackbed telling its own story. After examining the station my friend decided to walk down the trackbed to find the tunnel which he had heard about. He walked into the cutting and saw the mouth of the tunnel ahead; it was a very straight tunnel and he could see the bright sunlight at the end of the bore. He decided to go in and explore; the track had been removed but the entrances hadn't been sealed yet. Consulting his notes, he discovered that the tunnel was nearly half a mile long. He ventured in, the sound of his footfalls on the still existent ballast was somewhat reassuring; he was conscious of the darkness as he progressed further into the tunnel.

Now and again, he paused and looked back to the receeding sight of the old station; then he looked ahead to the welcoming arc of sunlight at the other end of the tunnel; the sound of water dripping from the vaulted brick roof was rhythmic and evocative.

He had been progressing steadily for perhaps ten minutes when suddenly he became aware of another presence in the tunnel. He stopped and listened; only the constant drip of water, sometimes near at hand, sometimes distant, broke the silence.

Then my friend's hair rose on the back of his neck as a figure flitted from one side of the tunnel to the other. Passing the bright arc of sunlight, it was unmistakable; it happened; he saw it. It made no sound, which was strange as the ballast had echoed my friend's footsteps. The figure was now lost in the shadows of the tunnel; was it hiding in a manhole? Or was it waiting in stealth to strike him? He stopped walking and peered into the stygian darkness. All manner of thoughts crowded his mind; what was the figure up to? Was it scavenging, or just some youth trying to frighten someone?

There was no sign of movement now and no light which was stranged as anyone searching in the corners of this tunnel would need some sort of illumination. At this stage my friend hadn't thought of the supernatural; besides he didn't believe in that sort of thing . . . He looked back to the station end of the tunnel; it seemed a long way back. There was no sign of the figure, so he decided to go on a bit further, only to find that his legs would not move forward. He tried again; it was as if an invisible barrier was holding him back. He was really afraid now, and he decided to beat a dignified retreat. He turned and walked slowly back, his legs working perfectly. Just to assure himself, he again turned round and tried to go the other way. He was doing well when all of a sudden he came up against the invisible barrier again. He picked up a piece of ballast and threw it; he watched the stone disappear into the darkness then, 'boing', he ducked as he heard it hit something. It was no good, he would have to get out of the strange placed – once in the daylight, common sense would return.

It seemed a long way back to the cutting and station; he was sweating in his haste and he sat down on a low wall to think things out. He had been taking photographs before he entered the tunnel and he was certain that he hadn't seen anyone enter the tunnel, yet . . .

Admittedly he had only had a brief glimpse of the figure but it had made a lasting impression; he couldn't understand the events which seemed to have no logical explanation. Any other person in the tunnel at that time would have betrayed their presence by the sound of their footfalls on the thick ballast on the tunnel floor. As a matter of interest my friend has spoken to other people who have ventured into the depths of Sharpthorne Tunnel and they too have had a very strong feeling of being watched by something.

The paranormal seemed to have been at work; mystifying and tantalising the mortal that dared to venture into the darkness and damp gloom. Was the sinister figure a former casualty of some railway disaster who returns to the scene of the accident? So far no explanation has been offered.

90

THE SINISTER SUITCASE

This story concerns not a ghost, but a baffling mystery which I believe has never been solved to this day, and its implications are horrific and unpleasant.

The police in the 1920s did not have the forensic skills or the facilities that they have today to help them in their task of bringing criminals to justice, news did not travel so fast in those days, and life was certainly more relaxed, but of course determination and dedicated application to every problem was still the hallmark of police work.

The story tells of a mystery which suggests that a savage murder had taken place. It was related to me some time ago and, as my informant does not wish to be identified, I will call her simply Mrs Jones.

The gas lamps flickered in the slight breeze that stirred the night air as I stood with my mother on the platform of Harrogate Station on a dark and dismal night in the early 1920s.

Suddenly out of the gloom a man appeared beside us carrying a large suitcase. His face was partly covered by a scarf and the upturned collar of his long black raincoat and he wore a shapeless trilby hat which had seen better days. 'Are you waiting for the Leeds train?' he asked in a well modulated but somewhat husky voice; my mother answered in the affirmative.

About five minutes later the tank engine hauling the Leeds

train clanked into the station, wheezed to a halt and stood simmering. We climbed into a compartment occupied by a lady and gentleman, my mother put our modest luggage on the luggage rack and we settled down on the dusty seats. A porter came along slamming doors and calling 'All stations to Leeds', then the carriage door was opened and the man with the suitcase who had spoken to us appeared, thrust the suitcase at our feet and melted into the night.

My mother looked at the case, a puzzled frown on her face. 'Does this case belong to you?' she asked the lady and gentleman. They stared at us and shook their heads. 'Why, isn't it yours?' the gentleman asked, surprised. My mother replied that it had nothing to do with us and glared at the large case as if it were an object of menace. The train started up, gathered speed and rattled into the night. The gentleman spoke up again. 'I say, what a strange turn up. Fancy leaving a thing like that – perhaps someone is picking it up at Leeds. I'll tell the guard when we stop.'

We all eyed the case with deepest suspicion as if it would suddenly open up and attack us. Then I swallowed my fear and tried to see through the dusty window, but all I could make out was the reflection of the others in the compartment.

The lady spoke. 'There was something in the papers last week, about a case being found at a railway station and later on when someone opened it they found a dismembered body inside . . . a human body.' I shuddered and moved c   : to my mother, who pursed her lips and frowned. 'What a thing to discuss. How horrible. I prefer not to think of such things.'

We now all gazed at the case with horror. What if it contained a body or the remains of a body? We moved our feet away as far as possible.

'We will be stopping at Pannal shortly; perhaps we can get rid of it there,' suggested the gentleman. 'I shall put it off there, I shall.' He looked at us all and glared.

As the train drew into Pannal my mother lowered the window and called the porter. He looked amazed as mother told him the story but to our relief took the suitcase, somewhat gingerly, and departed. We all sighed, looked at each other, and smiled. Had we worried unnecessarily? Were we premature in our wild thoughts? As the worry slipped off our minds we spent the rest of the journey speculating on what could have been in the sinister suitcase. Did it contain a dismembered body? Or the proceeds of a robbery? Would we ever know?

At last the train drew into Leeds and came to a halt. My mother and I stepped out on to the platform, gathered our luggage, said goodbye to our travelling companions and then I turned to look up at the station clock. As I turned my head my eye caught a glimpse of a tall man in a black raincoat wearing a scarf, his collar turned up, a battered trilby pulled down over his eyes coming towards us clutching a large suitcase . . .

91

THE MYSTERY OF THE SAD LADY

I am greatly indebted to Mr Gordon Nash of Aylesbury, Bucks, for his detailed account of an incident on a London tube train in January 1983, for which there would seem to be no rational explanation.

Let Mr Nash take up the tale.

I am a building surveyor by profession and, as a result of my work, I have had occasion to visit a considerable number of places where one might expect to find things a little beyond the realms of human comprehension.

I do find that some places and buildings have a 'feel', in most cases it is welcoming and homely, but sometimes the opposite feeling will occur. Usually I put these feelings down to my own imagination which has been influenced by memories of stories and yarns that could connect with a particular style of building or environment, but the strange thing about the incident that we are concerned with is that it took place in the heart of busy, dirty London, not in a lonely country house or remote countryside.

Before 1982 most of my work had been in Buckinghamshire and Hertfordshire, but during that year my employers moved into Victoria in central London. As I had no wish to move into the city, I became one of the faceless thousands who commute into London. Luckily I only had to go to the office two or three times a week, for the property owned by my employers was mostly in the home counties.

My journey to work involved catching a train from Aylesbury to Marylebone and then using the underground.

The underground journey involved catching a train from Marylebone to Oxford Circus using the old Bakerloo line. I used to then change trains at Oxford Circus and take a Victoria line train down to Victoria and then walk to the office.

For the most part, the journey I have just mentioned is very uninteresting. I used to leave home early in the morning to catch the 7am train from Aylesbury, and the winter mornings were the worst, with the rain streaming down the dirty windows of the ageing DMU, nothing to see except the blank expressions of my travelling companions. Once again I might have expected something unusual on this part of the journey as it involves travelling over the old Metropolitan Railway that used to terminate at Verney Junction. The line was also part of the once-impressive Great Central Railway but, alas, the great days of the line have declined, and it is now run with the commuter cattle truck methods employed to get so many people in and out of London.

It was on one of those winter mornings during January 1983 that an event occurred that has left me wondering ever since. It was wet and very cold and dawn had just broken as the train pulled into Marylebone. I remember lingering for a while in the compartment to get my coat and briefcase as I had no real wish to dash out into the cold and wet. The day was going to be one of those gloomy, dark days that make everything in London take on the colour of cold wet steel. I made my way to the southbound Bakerloo line; most of the first rush of passengers had caught a previous train and I managed to get a seat on the ageing 'rattler'.

The trip to Oxford Circus was uneventful and, like many who use the underground, I switched off and gazed into nothing. Changing from the southbound Bakerloo to the southbound Victoria at Oxford Circus is a shock for you step down from the old red rolling stock so familiar to those who knew the London underground during the 1930s and 40s into the 1970s' and 80s' world of silver trains and well-lit platforms.

However, still in my standard commuter daze, I got on to the southbound Victoria train which, for one reason or another, was almost empty. I had selected a coach close to the front of the train since, when the train stops at Victoria, the exit to the main line station is at the far end of the platform near the driver's compartment. I relaxed slightly in the marginally more comfortable surroundings and as the train pulled out of Oxford Circus I took my paper from my case to finish reading an article that I had started on the main-line train.

Our train was gaining speed rapidly and the rocking motion made reading difficult, so I decided to survey my fellow passengers. I often did this to pass the time. I used to try to guess what they did for a living – just a quick glance so as not to cause any embarrassment. A banker? A clerk? I would never know, but it provided mild amusement to break the boredom.

On this occasion there were no more than a dozen people in the whole coach. I had decided what one or two of them were, when I was struck by a young woman sitting diagonally across the compartment from me, just the other side of the exit doors. She was wearing a full-length dark blue coat buttoned into the neck and on her lap was a large soft black handbag. However, it was not her dress that caused me to glance back at her, it was the expression on her face. She had dark hair tied back, dark eyes and attractive, slim features, but she looked ill: her complexion was pale and there was very little colour in her cheeks; she had dark rings under her eyes and she stared into space as the train sped along. I looked back at my paper not wanting to make her uneasy, but I could not take my mind off that sad but so beautiful face.

Her expression mirrored the weather of the day – grey, overcast and damp, imbued with deep despair.

As anyone who travels the Victoria line will know there is only one station between Oxford Circus and Victoria and that is Green Park. I looked up as the train pulled out of Green Park Station and noticed that the young lady was still seated in the same position. In fact she did not appear to have moved a muscle and the pallor remained as did the look of despair. I turned back to my newspaper to overcome my feelings which were beginning to reflect the young woman's.

I felt the familiar braking of the train as we approached Victoria and heard the thunder of another train on the northbound line. At a point just before the station the northbound and southbound tunnels operate in what looks like a single bore, and a train running in the opposite direction is often seen. This has always been my signal to stand up and make my way to the doors. As I stood up I noticed that the sad young lady had left her seat but she was not standing by the doorway closest to both of us. In fact, I was the only person in that doorway. I thought that perhaps I had distressed her with my glances and I felt a little guilty about that.

I looked down the train towards the single door at the front of the compartment expecting to see her standing near that exit. There were one or two people there but no sign of her. I was certain that no one had passed in front of me heading toward the rear of the compartment to use the other two sets of doors, but I looked anyway. Again, one or two people stood by the exits, but not the lady.

The train drew into the station and ground to a halt with the usual squeal of brakes and hiss of compressed air as the pneumatic doors rolled back. By now I was puzzled. Where had my strange travelling companion gone? I should add here that at no time during this strange sequence of events did I feel fear or unease. I looked up and down the platform just to satisfy my curiosity, but to no avail. It was not that the platform was crowded, but the few people who left the train did not seem to be in any hurry to reach street level and the cold winter air.

I even looked up and down the escalator as I ascended – nothing, other than the faceless crowd that I normally formed part of, no sign of the pale young lady in the blue coat.

What I think now to be the truth began to dawn on me.

Had I seen a ghost? And what would a ghost be doing on the 8.10am Victoria line southbound out of Oxford Circus?

Sometimes on cold winter's evenings when travelling home on the main-line train, watching the water droplets run down the dirt of the window and looking at my own grey reflection against the blackness behind the glass, I wonder who my ghost was and why she looked so much like a cold, grey, winter morning in London.

I have nothing to support my story, but I have nothing to gain by relating it. You may take it that it actually happened.

92

THE MIDLAND BRAKE VAN

It is not difficult to imagine weird, and sometimes inexplicable 'happenings' and visitations in isolated places such as dark and wet railway tunnels, remote signal boxes lit only by the flickering oil lamps throwing emotive shadows everywhere, or the gas-lit rural station, deserted yet atmospheric, the silent empty platforms seeming to recall passengers who have passed and are now part of the great unknown; even deep railway cuttings conjure up an aura of mystique.

It is of course only too true that some of these places just mentioned have been the scene of tragic accidents and the past often clings to scenes of accidents.

One such story concerns an unexplained 'visitation' which occurred in an old Midland Railway brake van many years ago, in fact shortly after the railway grouping in the early 1920s. To the unenlightened, the interior of a brake van at night, lit only by the guard's hand lamp and the intermittent flames from the opened flap of the stove, would be so full of flickering shadows, emotive shapes and ethereal, mystical patterns as to perhaps unnerve even the most strong-willed creature.

The story of what happened to goods guard Edwin Carter, in charge of the old Midland brake van working back to Grimsby from Stainforth one cold winter's night, was told to me by his nephew Clive who, on his retirement from South African Railways where he had been employed as a freight foreman, was on a visit to his home town.

Uncle Edwin, Clive had to admit, was a bit of a character, and he had 'been around' a lot, but of all the stories he told, and there were many, the tale about this particular trip in the old Midland brake van was one that he swore was true and totally unexplained. Even Clive was impressed by the serious-ness of his old uncle's voice and demeanour when relating the happenings that night so many years ago.

However, let Clive tell the story and then we can make up our own minds.

Immingham goods guard Edwin Carter had signed on one night at 9.30pm at the empty sidings guard's room. Then, having been told where his train of coal empties stood, he opened his locker and took out his large leather bag and his hand lamp, then went outside and into the adjoining lamproom to trim his lamp. Then he walked down his train to examine the couplings and to pick up any handbrakes that might have dropped down as the trains were shunted. Reaching his brake van he was pleased to see that it was a good GCR one and not one of those old rough-riding former Midland ones that were somehow still being used. He lit his two side lamps and tail lamp, put some coal on the stove which had been lit for him by the yard foreman and walked back down the other side of the train to repeat his examination. He stood at the head of the train to await the arrival of the train engine but did not have to wait long and as it backed up carefully he watched it buffer up, then removed the engine tail lamp to save the fireman the job. As he climbed up the steps to the footplate the driver greeted him. 'Hello Edwin, how many have we got on tonight?' 'Only 35,' he replied.

The fireman offered him a cup of tea from his brew can which Edwin accepted gratefully. 'Whistle up when you're ready Fred,' he said to the driver. 'Draw up when the "Peg" comes off and I'll get in.' Minutes later he was in the brake van and they were on their way.

It was an uneventful trip for them to Stainforth, arriving and being relieved on time. In the old converted carriage messroom in the sidings they joined other train crews waiting their turn to work home. After about an hour Edwin was told that their train was next up and would be arriving in minutes, so they gathered up their things and went outside to wait.

They didn't have long to wait and as their train came into view headed by one of the splendid ex-GCR 2–8–0 'Supers', he proceeded to walk down the line past the oncoming train to relieve the guard. The coal train came slowly past and he looked up to see to his disgust that the brake was one of the detested ex-Midland Railway 'Rough Riders'. Edwin stood waiting for it to approach and come to a stand. He saw the train guard clamber down and greet him. 'Hello mate. You've got 30 on for West Marsh, a single load and you're in for a rough trip – the bloody thing rocks and rolls all over the place and it is cold and draughty, although I've tried to build the fire up for you.'

Edwin climbed up into the brake and went inside. He looked twice at the huddled-up figure opposite the guard's seat adjacent to the big brake wheel. Whoever it was was evidently asleep and Edwin thought it was unusual that the other guard had not mentioned that Edwin had company for the ride home. After all, it was nothing very strange for train crews to ride home in the brakes on occasions. However he was not too bothered and went outside on the verandah to wait for the driver to whistle up to signal their departure. On hearing the whistle he held his hand lamp out and waited for the whistle blast of acknowledgement then went back inside the brake, sitting down on his seat opposite his travelling companion.

He could see little of the man in the dim interior but could make out a uniform coat and a shiny peaked cap. Edwin thought, I'll not disturb him till we get to Gunness; he might be a Scunthorpe guard, passing Thorne North. He went through his usual routine, going outside on the verandah to look at his train to see if there was anything untoward such as signs of hot boxes, but apart from the odd spark of a swinging brake block here and there coming into contact with a wheel, which was quite normal, everything was all right.

260

Going back inside the brake, he was about to sit down for a few minutes and have a few minutes 'shuteye' when he noticed, with a shock, that he was alone – his travelling companion had gone. Whatever had happened? The brake van front door was still secured, with a wedge under the door bottom to make it fast in the door frame, so he could not have gone out that way. Edwin began to have doubts. Had the man existed? Could it have been a trick of the shadows? Had he imagined it? He thought hard. He had seen the uniform and the shiny cap – the figure had been real all right.

For the rest of the journey, despite of being bounced and banged by the corkscrew motion of the brake, Edwin could not take his mind off the experience. A rational man, he did not like mysteries; to him everything was black or white, there were no grey areas of vague unexplained theories.

He looked hard at the seat on the other side of the brake that his 'companion' had seemed to occupy and he willed the 'ghost' or whatever it was to materialise again, but nothing happened. As if it would, he thought. I must be getting old or prematurely senile; perhaps I have been dreaming. The crowded thoughts took his mind off everything until with a lurch he realised that they had arrived at West Marsh Sidings and he would now leave the old brake van with its inexplicable 'presence' to someone else.

When the train came to a halt he wound down the brake wheel and climbed down on to the ballast. He walked down the train to the engine and uncoupled between the tender and train then clambered up on to the footplate. 'Had a good ride Edwin?' asked the driver. Edwin grimaced. 'Rotten, not your fault though. I was shaken up and banged about but I've arrived here in one lump so I can't grumble too much. But I'll tell you this, I never want to see that brake again. I've got its number and I'll take good care that I'll never ride in it again.' Edwin decided not to tell the driver and fireman about the queer figure because he would only get his leg pulled.

As he left to go home he could not resist going to have a look at the old Midland brake van again.

261

The moon had appeared from behind scudding clouds, briefly lighting up the scene and the solidness of the van seemed curiously ominous as he approached. Then he spotted something, he stopped in his tracks and his mouth fell open. There on the verandah was a dark figure. It was in the shadow of the verandah's overhang but it was there. Edwin ran forward, convinced that some one was having a joke but, as he got nearer, to his amazement the figure melted into the night and the moon was again obscured by the night clouds.

About a year later, when talking to a Stainforth guard, he mentioned the experience. It appeared that this guard had also seen the mysterious 'passenger' on one occasion, and it was assumed that it was the ghost of a guard who had died in the brake van some years earlier whilst travelling home. Evidently the Stainforth men knew all about the apparition but were not unduly concerned about the phantom passenger who travelled home with an earthly colleague.

93

THE STORY OF THE
PHANTOM WESTERN

I am grateful to Mr G. Heathcliffe of Swindon for his account of the baffling reappearance of a Western class diesel hydraulic locomotive which was seen again after its demise at the hands of the dismantlers at Swindon Works.

Mr Heathcliffe is a railwayman. I suppose he would be referred to as a devoted Western diehard, his main love during their reign being the Western class locomotives that dominated the expresses from 1961 until the mid 1970s. His favourite loco in the class was D1042 *Western Princess*, and he was very disappointed when he was told that D1042 was being withdrawn from service in the July of 1973 and would be scheduled to be cut up in January 1974.

British Railways were rationalising their motive power and the diesel-hydraulic locos such as the Western and Hymek classes were to be withdrawn as the stock of spare parts would be difficult to obtain. Another reason may have been that the availability of such locomotives was uneven, and the proposed new image of the 'Super' trains. HST 125s and the electrification of many lines added to the demise of the hydraulics and ultimately the deltics would share the same fate. They call it progress.

Mr Heathcliffe went with his father to Newbury races on a cold, but sunny day in mid-May 1974. Mr Heathcliffe junior did not particularly like horses but the racecourse at Newbury

263

was situated very near the main railway line to the West of England so he thought he would see something interesting during the day out.

However, for the first hour of watching the line only class 47 locomotives were in charge of the trains to and from Paddington, but eventually the unmistakable sound and shape of a Western came into view. He could clearly see the number and name: it was D1041 *Western Prince* hauling well-filled coaches and it was in good fettle doing about 80mph. Following the train down he saw the blue sky darken and heard again the familiar 'Maybach music' (as the noise of Western class engines is known to enthusiasts). Another Western was approaching. From round the curve came a shiny, highly polished Western singing sweetly as only a well-maintained machine can.

As she drew level with him he could read very clearly the name and number, *Western Princess* D1042. Deep joy. His favourite engine had been reprieved and repaired. This kind of practice by British Railways was not unknown, withdrawn locomotives being taken out of store and overhauled and put back into service mainly due to shortage of motive power.

However, a few days later a friend in Swindon Works said, 'I've got bad news for you. We cut your old friend *Princess* up on the 18th.' 'Oh no you didn't,' replied Mr Heathcliffe. 'I saw her on an up express at Newbury that day, so pull the other one.' His friend persisted, but it was not until Mr Heathcliffe saw the fact in print that he actually believed that *Western Princess* was no more.

So what did he see at Newbury on 18 May 1974? He repeats that, as a railwayman, he knew what the locomotive looked like, even if he is a railway enthusiast! The shape and sound of a Maybach-engined Western is unique and the only other Western it could have been was *Western Prince* and that had been seen moments before going in the other direction. Could he have witnessed the final fling of the *Western Princess* on the day she 'died' in the Swindon Works?

A similar kind of experience was witnessed by a colleague

one Saturday night in South Devon. He was heading east on an express between Plymouth and Totnes when it was stopped by engineering work. The locomotive on the engineers' train was D1067 *Western Druid*. Records show that this locomotive was cut up on 16th September 1976, and yet the sighting of the engine in question was noted in February 1977.

So what can we deduce from these experiences? Mr Heathcliffe is adamant that his story is factual and completely without fabrication. Maybe the sceptics will smile and show their scorn, but the people who understand these remarkable events will also smile their contentment.

94

RUNAWAY TRUCKS

Mr E. L. Anderson recalls an incident during the last war when he was in the RAF, stationed in Lincolnshire, as he travelled up by train from his home near Bedford.

One foggy Sunday night in February he caught a late train from an almost deserted Bedford station. As is often the case when one embarks from a dark lonely platform, he had the feeling as the train wound its way through the flat fog-shrouded countryside that he was the only one on the train. After gazing out of the misty and dirty windows of the compartment for a while he snuggled down in his greatcoat and dozed off to sleep.

The train normally took several hours to reach Lincoln, stopping and starting at frequent intervals, although nobody seemed to get on or off and no one joined him in his compartment.

Then the train came to a halt with a jolt that awakened him immediately and nearly deposited him on the carriage floor. He looked around, but he was still alone in the compartment. He could hear steam blowing off from the engine. Rubbing the misty window he peered through it, but could make out very little in the darkness outside. Plainly though, they were nowhere near a station. He sat for a while wondering what could have caused the sudden halt, then pulling the strap which released the window he slid it down. Putting his head out he gazed up and down the track. He could see nothing but fog-bound fields and a few lighted windows of the train he was in. Obviously he was not the only one on it, but nobody else seemed to be taking any notice of the stoppage.

Then he heard the crunch of running footsteps and a man appeared out of the mist near the front of the train. As he approached, Mr Anderson could see that the man was wearing what looked like the dark uniform of a railwayman and was waving his arms about. He appeared to be shouting something although it was not easy to make out what he was saying.

Then, as he drew near, his words came clear. 'Runaway trucks!' he was shouting in a hoarse voice. 'Runaway trucks!'

Then he had gone by and was running towards the end of the train, soon disappearing into the mist.

Almost immediately, the train jerked into motion and continued its slow progress. Mr Anderson sat back in his seat nonplussed. Why had the the train stopped suddenly, and just as suddenly started again? And who was the man running by the side of the track? What did he mean? Was there some danger? But nobody seemed bothered. The driver of the train was obviously proceeding, albeit at a slow pace, but seemed unconcerned by the running man. But there was nothing that Mr Anderson could do. He was in a compartment on his own, in a non-corridor train, unable to communicate with anybody.

The train arrived at Lincoln without further incident. A few people got out, mostly service personnel, and went in search of the RAF lorries lined up in the station yard which would take them to their respective camps in the county. Mr Anderson, still puzzled about what he had seen, joined them.

As he climbed aboard his own lorry he saw a group of friends. It appeared that they had travelled on the same train, although he had not seen them. They had also noticed the train stopping abruptly and though one or two had looked out none had seen the running railwayman or heard the shouted words.

He later made enquiries of all airmen he could find who had travelled on the train that night and discovered that he was the only one who had seen the running man or heard his shouts. After thinking about it for some time he eventually decided that he must have been half asleep when the train shuddered to a halt and imagined the rest of the incident.

Years later, however, he wondered . . . He read a newspaper account of some trucks which had broken free in a siding on the same line and smashed into a train coming the other way, killing the driver. Could he have seen something which was to happen in the future?

95

FOOTSTEPS AT PURLEY OAKS STATION

My correspondent, Mr R. L. P. Belanger, tells me a story about the mysterious phenomenon at Purley Oaks Station in Surrey.

Between 1962 and 1964 I was the leading porter at Purley Oaks Station between Purley and East Croydon on the main line to Brighton, although we only had local trains stopping there.

In November 1963 the Oaks was still lit by gas lamps which hissed and spluttered during the evening. To avoid hanging about after the last train departed we had worked out a system for closing down which went like this. The last Coulsdon North to Victoria train went at 10.45 so all lights on platform 1 were put out. At 11.08 the last Caterham to Charing Cross light on platform 3 plus the end lights on 2 and 3 were put out and the booking hall was locked up. All gates that had been collected were booked and the staff room was tidied up ready to lock up. My last Victoria to Coulsdon North train arrived at about 11.50 and the remainder of the island platform lights were put out, after which I returned to the staff room and locked up before meeting the last train. At 12.05 I crossed the station to deal with the last train, the 12.08 (if I remember correctly) from Charing Cross to Tattenham Corner, Caterham, an eight-car train. Purley Oaks platform 4 was built for three-car sets and only took six coaches, so the leading porter had to stand at the London end, to make sure there were no passengers for the Oaks.

On the occasion in question nobody alighted so, after giving the 'all clear' to the guard, the train left. I then proceeded with my pole to put out the remaining lights, three at each end and two under the canopy and the waiting room. After putting out the London end and the canopy and waiting room, I started on the last three, walking toward the signal. After putting out the first light I heard footsteps on the stairs which lead from the subway to the platform. Having to return that way I ignored them until between the last two lights, with the footsteps getting closer, I turned round to offer whoever it was a lift into Purley. But there was nobody there and yet the footsteps kept on coming towards me.

I turned and fled across four lines neither looking left nor right. I threw my helmet on my head, put my greatcoat on the seat of my scooter and ran it until it started, jumped on and was gone, leaving stairway and subway lights still on.

I do not know who or what had followed me on platform 4 and I didn't care – I just went.

It is only fair to mention that platform 4 is on stilts but it was no echo, as the footsteps continued long after I had stopped moving.

During the following week I asked my opposite leading porter, John Fitch, if he had heard or seen anything on late turn and he told me that he had also heard footsteps on occasions.

I later transferred to Kenley Station and John went to work for National Carriers.

I can assure you that every word of my story is absolutely true.

96

HIBALDSTOW CROSSING

Some signal boxes and crossing keeper's cabins are, by virtue of their locations, very lonely and sometimes very frightening places. These structures are usually warm in winter and cool in the summer, but on a wild winter's night when the gales are blowing, the creaks and the movement and the many mysterious noises of the night can make the occupants feel rather ill at ease and wonder if they are really alone . . .

Picture then the lonely gate keeper's cabin situated just by the A15 road in North Lincolnshire near Brigg. Hibaldstow Crossing is the name of the location; the cabin and a small house are the only signs of life.

In the 1920s, when transport was just beginning to become mechanised, the horse and trap was still a popular means of going from A to B if you were travelling locally. The crossing keeper's cabin was a little wooden hut close by the railway line and the gates across the road. The gates were of course hand operated and the indicators in the cabin passed the instructions from the nearest signal box, telling the crossing keeper that a train was on the way. The little cabin was rather basic: we have mentioned the indicators, and there was also a small coke stove which gave some warmth, but with the door open so often the heat was quickly lost.

However, in the mid-1920s an accident happened that caused a man to lose his life still. It would appear that his restless spirit still visits the scene of the tragedy.

It so happened that the crossing keeper at Hibaldstow (who

lived at the Crossing cottage) had been taken ill suddenly and so was unable to perform his duties. In view of this a porter named Kirkman who worked at Hibaldstow and Scawby Station was sent to cover the duty at the remote Hibaldstow Crossing, but subsequent events were to reveal the folly of sending an inexperienced man to do this job, and the man's apparent ignorance of the finer points of the operation was to cost him his life.

The ultimate act that cost Mr Kirkman his life was quite simple. He was given the information on the cabin indicator and was struggling to open one of the gates, having successfully managed to open the other one, when he was run down by the approaching train.

The subsequent inquest duly returned a verdict of death by accident and the whole unfortunate incident was deemed to be closed. Operations returned to normal, but with extra emphasis on safety.

However, later events suggest that poor Mr Kirkman returned to the scene of the accident because crossing keepers spoke of hearing footsteps near the cabin. Investigation revealed nothing but my contributor, Mr G. Coverdale, who now lives in Scunthorpe and who worked as crossing keeper at Hibaldstow Crossing, has heard the sounds of the footsteps on several occasions and will vouch for the truth of the stories.

Mr Coverdale was very puzzled and frightened at the time and at first put it down to anything but a paranormal experience, but after several occurrences of the kind he began to believe that there was a ghost. No shape was ever seen but the solid-sounding footsteps approaching the cabin were enough to frighten some of Mr Coverdale's workmates who were certainly not keen on working the night shift. When anyone heard the strange noise, they would automatically search the area immediately around the cabin for the reason but none was forthcoming. The supernatural was at work in all its mystery. To find everything was a practical joke would have been a welcome relief but no such hoax was the reason for the sounds in the middle of the night.

Other members of the shift give slightly varying accounts of their experiences but they all insist on having heard footsteps and can offer no explanation for them. They all looked around outside the cabin without any result, and there was never anyone there.

With the installation of automatic barriers in 1966 the crossing became unmanned. Gone was the gateman and the little old cabin; gone too were the unexplained sounds of the phantom footsteps for there were no gatemen to feel the hair rise on the back of the neck as the measured tread approached the cabin. But people remember the lonely crossing keeper crouched in the little cabin waiting for the sound of the indicator to warn him of an approaching train, and they remember the dreaded sound of the footsteps and the howling of the wind across the winter landscape.

97

THE GHOST OF FAIR BECCA

A terrifying experience witnessed by an unsuspecting teenager was passed on to me by Mr P. Briggs of Bradford.

The location for this strange and bizarre event was the Horton branch line. This line no longer exists but it ran from Keighley to Queensbury where it was joined by a line from Halifax as it descended to Clayton, Great Horton, Horton Park, St Dunstans and then terminated at Bradford Exchange Terminus. The Keighley and Worth Valley people refer to it as the 'GN' (Great Northern).

The story is as follows.

A young man who lived in the village of Clayton and worked in one of the textile mills at Great Horton used to travel on the railway to work and back when he could afford it. At other times he had to walk, for pay in those days was not a lot and he had to be careful. On Fridays he received his week's pay so he could buy himself fish and chips at teatime and he would then perhaps go on to one of the local picture houses, maybe the Plaza or the Grange or the Elysian, after which he would catch the train home. As this story is set in the 1940s the only other form of transport in the Bradford area was the trams.

One icy winter's night at Great Horton when the moon lit up the landscape with its translucent glow the young man waited for the two-coach train to arrive. He was cold and stamped his feet to try to keep warm. Eventually the train chugged into view. A tank engine was the motive power, running bunker first, and the young man noticed that there were very few passengers on board.

He got on to the train and quickly found an empty compartment. In a few minutes the guard gave the right of way, the engine whistled and the train steamed slowly out of the station.

The windows of the compartment were shrouded in vapour as the engine worked hard on the incline towards Clayton.

Just beyond the station the line runs through a cutting and under a road bridge (Old Corn Lane), which is midway in the cutting, to a footbridge at the end of the embankment to Clayton Station.

As the train passed through the cutting the compartment suddenly went icy cold and the steam from the engine cleared, revealing a woman's face pressed against the window pane. For no apparent reason the sounds of the train died but the ghastly twisted face of the woman was still glued to the window. It was horrible: it was as if she was trying to get into the train. For what seemed an age the young man cowered in a corner of his seat frozen with terror, his eyes wide open with the shock.

Then, as suddenly as the face had appeared, it vanished. The sounds of the train's movements came back and the train steamed into Clayton Station. The young man staggered out of the train, his face ashen, and almost collapsed into the arms of the guard. He blurted out his story and the guard nodded sympathetically . . . he'd heard it all before . . . the young man had seen the ghost of Fair Becca.

It seems that Becca was having an affair with another man, but her husband found out and killed her, then threw her body down a well near Brackenhill Park. The ghost of Becca is said to haunt the area along the railway line. Apparently her spectre is well known and has been seen on many occasions in recent years. So if anyone fancies seeing it they should trace the old track bed of the line around dusk or late at night when the moon is full and the owls call 'Beware of Fair Becca'.

98

STRANGE HAPPENINGS AT
WEBB HOUSE

I have often been asked awkward questions about my collections of railway ghost stories, the main one being 'How do you explain it?' People will always try to find a logical explanation.

The answer is of course that there is no explanation for a supernatural event. People have been probing the intricacies of the paranormal for hundreds of years without any acceptable conclusions emerging.

Some people are able to experience paranormal events; others are totally unable to. So we have the believer and non-believer, the feelings of each as strong as the experiences themselves.

I met such differing opinions when I tried to investigate the strange happenings at Webb House in Victoria Avenue, Crewe. I was told this house was the setting for phantom dogs and the sound of children's voices. But where does Webb House fit into a book of railway ghost stories?

Francis William Webb was chief superintendent engineer of the London North Western Railway from 1871 to 1903. Webb House was named after him, was at one time an orphanage for the children of railwaymen and is now a training school for railway staff, hence the connection with railways.

I received a letter from a Mr H. C. Johnston from Liverpool suggesting that I investigate the alleged happenings in this old building. Mr Johnston mentioned the phenomena above, and also the sounds of footsteps on the upper floor.

Seeking further information I wrote to British Rail at Webb House asking for any details that might exist to substantiate the stories I had been told. Their reply was disappointing: they denied that anything untoward had ever happened, just as an unbeliever would. After all we do not all have the opportunity of seeing signs of the other world, and the writer was frank and sensible. That's it I thought, end of story.

However, about six months later, to my surprise, I received a letter from a Mrs Fox who is the wife of the caretaker who looks after Webb House. The Fox family live in a cottage in the grounds and have had several very mystifying experiences both in Webb House and the cottage.

Mrs Fox had apparently read in the local newspaper my letter asking for further material for volume two of my railway ghosts book (now encompassed in this edition) and her story turned out to be very mystifying. Her letter provided plenty of details on her family's experiences in and around Webb House.

Mrs Fox describes herself as a practising Christian, feet firmly on the ground and sensible. Her story unfolds as follows:

Many years ago, during one particularly cold Saturday evening, my family, comprising husband, young son and two little girls were watching television in our sitting room at Webb Cottage. I was preparing the evening meal and because the cottage was so cold I decided to let them eat in front of the television and enjoy the warmth of the fire. I had carried the cutlery and plates into the room and was returning through the dining room with a tray containing the children's food. As I passed the fireplace I stepped over the extended paws of a large black dog who was lying in front of the fire. When I entered our sitting room I was surprised as our own Great Dane bitch 'Lisa' was lying with our younger daughter in front of the fire. 'Lisa' was a brindle colour, definitely not black. My husband, seeing my startled expression, asked me what was the matter. I hurriedly gave him the tray and shot back into the dining room, but the large black dog had gone! Since then I have seen the black dog only twice in sixteen years, but both occasions have left an impression. I *have* seen him and he is a happy dog; my husband has also seen him and corroborates my experience.

At weekends my husband goes into the main building of Webb House to check that there have been no break ins or intruders, and in the winter, no burst pipes. In the winter months I usually go with him and on one occasion we both heard the sound of a child crying. Very distinct, the cries seemed to be those of a young girl and to be coming from the attic suite. We went up there to investigate, but there was no sign of the cries or a child, we had a good look round, expecting to find signs of a break in (you know what kids are). Nothing was found to evoke a reason. My husband was annoyed that the reason for the strange noises was not readily explained; he didn't like mysteries!

We were to hear the sounds on many other occasions, but after thorough searches, nothing could be found. My husband, to his chagrin and worry, has also seen the figure of a well-built gentleman, dressed in a dark suit with either knickerbockers or breeches, long hair, a beard and a vague white cravat. This figure has been seen several times by various people.

Mrs Fox emphasises that she has recalled the experiences of herself and husband. She strenuously maintains that the truth has been uppermost at all times and that neither she or her husband were actually frightened or disturbed by the events, though they accept that there would appear to be no logical explanation for the strange happenings at Webb House.

Another example of the veil being lifted to reveal the past, or is it?

99

MY OLD FRIEND

This story was taken from *Weekend Magazine* of 4–10 April 1979.

My friend Bernie Marks was tall, dark and handsome. He came from a wealthy family and he had a remarkable capacity for drink, mostly spirits, which I shared in those days before the war.

Bernie had a Mercedes-Benz motor car and it seemed that the more he drank the better he drove. Never having seen him quite sober, I used to wonder if he could manage to drive a car without a drink inside him.

We lived in Manchester in those far-off days and enjoyed our evenings out together until I got married and gave up running around with the boys.

I settled down to a quiet family life, just as a married man should, but I heard that Bernie was still continuing his high life, a real 'good-time boy'.

When the war started Bernie joined up, even though he could have been exempted as the managing director of a firm working on government contracts.

As it was, he found himself driving important officers round London. I wondered about his drinking and driving.

Because of a World War I wound I was exempt and I had a job as a manager of a clothing factory, plus my civil defence duties.

By 1945 I had three children and my boss offered an all-expenses-paid holiday for them and my wife as a bonus for my hard work. They set off to the best hotel in Blackpool for a fortnight and I was allowed two long weekends with them.

One Monday morning I caught the early train from Blackpool to Manchester to get back to work. As we approached Manchester's Victoria Station another train pulled alongside. I was sitting by the window and suddenly I saw my old friend Bernie Marks in the train opposite. I was astonished because he looked so pale and ill and his eyes were staring out of his window into space, but there was no doubt it was Bernie. I let my window down and waved to him as our trains moved side by side.

By now we were quite close and I shouted his name as loud as I could, but he just stared blankly into space seemingly oblivious of my frantic efforts to attract his attention.

Bernie's train swerved away and I said to a passenger in my compartment, 'That's my oldest friend I was waving to.'

To my surprise the stranger replied, 'I didn't see anyone.' I said, 'Well I'll catch up with him at Victoria Station.' The stranger answered, 'No you won't; that train is going into Manchester Central.'

He was right so I went to the office intending to ring Bernie's home as soon as possible to arrange to meet up again, but pressure of work prevented my making the call.

It wasn't until the Friday that I decided to go to the old pub where Bernie drank, thinking he might be there. Instead his brother was there. 'How's Bernie?' I asked him.

'Don't you know?' he said. 'Bernie's dead; he was killed in a car crash last week in London.'

I was stunned. I heard Bernie's brother say, 'They brought his body back by train and we met the coffin at Central Station last Monday morning.'

With a chill I realised that I must have seen my old friend's ghost peering from the window of the train carrying his body home.

So he was in the train after all and only I could see him.

I didn't believe in ghosts then and I still have my doubts

280

. . . but I shall always believe in what I saw that morning.

There is a curious postscript to the story. The autopsy on Bernie showed that there was no alcohol in his body. It gave me a wry smile. I always knew Bernie could not drive well without a drink.

100

THE RETURN OF BINNS BANKCROFT

A few years ago, a volunteer railway enthusiast, who we will call Paul Smith, had journeyed to Haworth, on the Keighley and Worth Valley line that ran from Keighley to Oxenhope in Yorkshire.

Paul was keen to play his part in the restoration of trains and the gradual bringing back to life of the pleasant five-mile-long branch line. He lived in Lincolnshire and found difficulty getting over to Haworth very often, but the trip was always worth any difficulty. The interesting work of reclaiming the past and the challenge of operating the line as a tourist attraction spurred him on.

Some of the volunteers who came from afar would sleep in a sleeping coach in the goods yard at Haworth. From the coach one had a good view of the stone-walled yard and the adjacent road, though sometimes the view would be blocked by rolling stock that was stored in the yard and soon a new multi-purpose shed was to be built on the yard to remedy lack of covered space.

One summer night, after chatting to his mates about the day's events Paul decided to have a walk round the yard before turning in. The night was warm and almost windless, the paraphernalia of station equipment took up many corners of the yard and shadows were everywhere. Paul was pleasantly tired and content. He was not aware of anything untoward until before his eyes he caught a glimpse of something moving in the corner of the yard. Puzzled, he went forward to approach the area only to witness the hazy shape of an old wizened man holding a long pole. The figure seemed solid enough, but the haze made it difficult to discern the features. Paul froze to the spot, fascinated by the scene. The area where the man stood seemed to show other features as if of another background; part of the scene had altered. Paul felt compelled to play the part of observer, and as the figure moved about waving the long pole and gesturing, he started to move forward to get a better look at him, but as he approached the man seemed to melt away.

Paul ran back to the sleeping coach and as the sound of snoring told him that most of the inhabitants were asleep, he got into his bunk and lay awake turning over in his mind what he had seen in the yard. He wasn't frightened; he was more baffled. He certainly wasn't psychic and pooh-poohed the idea of ghosts. Sleep claimed him at last.

In the morning he couldn't wait to discuss the mystery with his mates. A good laugh was had by all, though this response didn't help his attempts to find a logical explanation for the events and he couldn't get the matter out of his mind all day.

A few days later he found himself talking to an old hand whose father had worked for British Rail at Haworth many years before. Paul mentioned his experience to him and he didn't seem at all surprised.

'It would be old Bankcroft you saw; he sometimes appears to have a look round', he said.

Paul nodded. 'I've heard of him in the last few days, but I thought it was some kind of joke.'

The old hand shook his head. 'Oh no, Binns Bankcroft thinks he still works in this yard'. And the old man told the story:

Binns Bankcroft was a coal merchant in Haworth in the latter part of the last century. His premises were located in the goods yard across the road from the railway station so he hadn't far to go to pick up his coal supply. When the coal was shunted into the yard Binns was always there to help, his shunting pole in his hand, and when the wagons had discharged their load, Binns would drive his horse and cart into the yard and load up for his local deliveries. He liked to be in the yard when the coal train arrived, and he would try to direct operations for shunting the wagons, bawling instructions to the engine driver and guard. They regarded him as a damn nuisance who did nothing but get in the way and cause many anxious moments for them as he darted in and out between the wagons. They feared for his safety, but he was always there and they could do nothing to keep him away from the station.

One winter's day in 1882 Binns was supervising operations as usual as the coal wagons were shunted into Haworth goods yard. He was waving his pole and bellowing instructions to the guard who was trying to understand his shouts in the high wind. Binns was a little hard of hearing so his replies to the driver and guard were also made difficult to comprehend – it was not surprising that problems would occur. Binns was moving in and around the wagons when, failing to heed the warning shouts of the guard, he was caught between two wagons and the life was crushed out of him. The subsequent inquest held at the nearby Royal Oak Inn returned a verdict of 'Death by Misadventure', so that was the end of Binns Bankcroft . . . or was it?

In 1968, Haworth Goods Yard was the scene of much activity when the Keighley and Worth Valley Preser-vation Society began operations to re-open the line. The goods shed was found to be very useful for repairs and attention to locomotives while the yard with its sidings was invaluable for storing stock of all kinds.

Preservation Society members who travel to work on the line at weekends often sleep in the sleeping coaches parked in one of the sidings in the yard, and they have many unexplained tales to tell. One night a man who was visiting the railway saw a light on in the goods shed. Thinking it was rare for anyone to be working as late as this hour he went to investigate, thinking someone had inadvertently left the light on. As he entered the old building everything was quiet and very still. The strange light seemed to be coming from the corner . . . a soft light, almost as if it were an oil lamp. Suddenly, the figure of a man emerged and walked towards him, a pole in his hand. Our friend was frozen to the spot and then, as suddenly as it had appeared, the figure melted in front of his astonished eyes.

To this day, various people swear that they have seen the ghost of Binns, and other people vouch for unexplained happenings in and around the goods shed. A lot of leg-pulling goes on regarding the sightings, but many are unshakeable in their belief that they have seen the shadow of the old man, and heard his footsteps in the yard which is now the scene of much activity as the Keighley and Worth Valley Preservation Society goes from strength to strength.

ACKNOWLEDGEMENTS

My grateful thanks to all those who helped me, in many ways, to formulate material for this book. I would particularly like to thank: C. Selway, H. Bunting, G. Nash, D. Duke, Mrs C. Barker, Mr G. Heathcliffe, Mr P. Briggs, Mrs E. Fox, Mr G. Coverdale, Mr D. Pearson, Mr R. Robinson (who gave legal advice when necessary), John McDonald, James Tomlinson, Tom McDevitte, Rev D. K. McKenzie, Peter Richardson, James Blake, Andrew Green, Fontana Books, Peter Underwood, Fontana/Collins Books, Jack Hayden, A. Dodsworth, Stuart Bailey, G. Knight, Ted Hudson, Derek Cross, Peter Handford, Observer newspaper, David Walker, D. Walker and D. Reynolds, John Rothera, Simon Winser, Durham County Library, M. Pritchett, PC 1405, H. B. Brookes, Peter Grant, Nick Matthews, John Daubney, Doris Jones-Baker, Collins Publishers, C. Barker, P. S. Chapman, B. J. Willey, J. J. Leslie, H. E. Caunt, C. E. Whitehead, H. C. Johnston, J. McIlmurray, J. Hallam, G. Leslie, R. J. Barry, P. Richardson, R. R. Mester, E. W. Poulter, Thorsons Publishing Group (Patrick Stephens Ltd), The Oxford Mail Newspaper Ltd, E. A. Shaw, R. J. Woodward, A. Dixon, M. A. Houghton, R. L. P. Belanger, P. Hussellbury, B. C. Essex, P. Craddock, D. M. Ross, J. Marshall, E. L. Anderson, D. Winn, M. Squires, A. Withnall, L. A. Whitehouse, P. Briggs, A. J. Ludlam, H. B. Brookes, B. Hamilton, C. Selway, I. McGill, P. Screeton, and all other sources of help, direct and indirect, and the help and encouragement of my friends. Thanks are also due to everyone else who gave advice and encouragement.

I would like to dedicate this book to my mother whose support was so vital.